How to Design and Build a Fireplace

ALSO BY STANLEY SCHULER:

Gardens Are for Eating

Gardening with Ease

Gardening in the East

Gardening from the Ground Up

America's Great Private Gardens

The Winter Garden

*All Your Home Building and
Remodeling Questions Answered*

*How to Design, Build, and Maintain
Your Swimming Pool*

The Complete Terrace Book

*How to Build Fences, Gates,
and Walls*

*5,000 Questions Answered
About Maintaining, Repairing, and
Improving Your Home*

How to

Design and Build a Fireplace

by Stanley Schuler

Macmillan Publishing Co., Inc.
New York

Collier Macmillan Publishers
London

Copyright © 1977 by Stanley Schuler

Macmillan Publishing Co., Inc.
866 Third Avenue, New York, N.Y. 10022
Collier Macmillan Canada, Ltd.

Library of Congress Cataloging in Publication Data

Schuler, Stanley.
How to design and build a fireplace.

1. Fireplaces—Design and construction.   I. Title.
TH7425.S37   697'.1   77-3331
ISBN 0-02-607360-9

First Printing 1977

Designed by Jack Meserole

Printed in the United States of America

Contents

How to Design and Build a Fireplace

1 Before You Build a Fireplace

For centuries, the fireplace was the only source of heat in the home. Then, when central heating arrived on the scene, the fireplace went into a decline. Whereas houses originally had three or four or even a half-dozen fireplaces, the great majority were reduced to only one. Many had no fireplaces at all.

Today the fireplace is enjoying a resurgence—a strong resurgence. And it's all because of the energy crisis. Millions of families who had mainly thought of the fireplace as a romantic feature of the house suddenly decided that it had functional value, too. Once again it is a heat source, a way of protecting the family pocketbook against those villainous Arabs, conniving oil companies, rapacious gas and electric utilities.

So it is. Whatever other virtues fireplaces have—and they have a number—we must never forget that it's the fire in the fireplace that counts.

At the same time, however, we must remember that a fireplace is a very inadequate heating system. I doubt that anyone has made a scientific study of how much heat a fireplace actually puts into a room. But it is a recognized fact that, of the total BTUs produced, only a small percentage warms the room and the people in it. The rest goes up the chimney.

This means that the wood burned in a fireplace is far from the bargain you may think it is. Not when it is selling for $75 a cord and up.

But I don't want to belabor this point. Put my negative comments down simply as a realistic aside. I just don't want anyone to build a fireplace in the expectation that it will keep him snug as a bug in a rug at dirt-cheap cost. It won't unless you have your own woodlot.

A fireplace will, however, cut your fuel bill for gas, oil or electricity a little if you keep a fire going steadily in cold weather. It will keep you comfortable on chilly spring and autumn nights that don't quite warrant turning on the furnace. It will—or at least it should—add to the beauty of the room in which it's located.

It will have a unifying effect on groups—pulling the individuals together, not only physically, but also mentally, thus promoting a

1

more cohesive feeling and greater understanding. It will foster marshmallow-roasting and popcorn-popping, with all the fun that attends such activities. It will even be used for broiling steaks.

A fireplace will have a calming, relaxing influence on bored, rambunctious children and equally bored, restless adults. In *The Human House*, Dorothy J. Field wrote:

During the winter months, when the children are often confined indoors for their play, it often happens that around four o'clock or a little after they become cross and grumpy in their playroom, or wild and almost hysterical with boredom. Then I light a fire in the living-room fireplace, and send the children in there to watch it; if the fire were not lighted they would continue their quarreling and perhaps try to turn the quiet room into another bedlam, but with the burning flames on the

The wall in which this large, low masonry fireplace is set serves as the divider between rooms. The flexible screen is designed so it can be pulled back beyond the sides of the fireplace, thus leaving the opening completely unobstructed.
(John Fulker)

hearth, they relax into easy interest. They see things in the fire, someone tells a story that interests the whole group, they quiet down, leaving me free to prepare the supper and serve it. It has a definitely hypnotic quality that can be turned to good account. The fireplace, therefore, while practically speaking it may be totally unnecessary in the modern home, may from the psychological point of view be a very definite tool in the management of children.*

Finally, a fireplace will provide infinite pleasure as you sit just watching the flames—flickering, leaping, changing color—and smell the rising smoke.

The fireplace has been derided as a sop to sentiment. A satisfier of primitive ritual. A phallic symbol. But there is no doubt that,

* Boston: Houghton Mifflin Co., 1939, p. 81.

whether it is a good source of heat or not, it is essential to most people.

The heart of the home.

To be perfectly mundane about it, why else do most real-estate ads bother to point out the "living room *with fireplace*"?

Whether you're building a new home, making an addition that will incorporate a fireplace or installing one in an existing house, there are a good many questions that must be answered before you actually start putting in the fireplace.

What Is the Principal Purpose of the Fireplace?

To provide warmth? Or to provide some of the intangible benefits described above?

If you're like most people, your answer is probably: "We want it to do both." And it will do both unless it's a stove, which is, with certain exceptions, primarily a heating unit. But don't settle for such a wishy-washy answer. If you really want the fireplace for heating, you must plan it accordingly.

There are four basic types of fireplace in use today:

1. The conventional masonry fireplace, which is custom-built brick by brick or stone by stone and which becomes a permanent part of the house.

2. The prefabricated built-in fireplace, which leaves the factory as a steel box and is permanently built into the house—usually without surrounding masonry. When completed, however, the fireplace is hard to distinguish from a conventional fireplace and heats the room in the same way.

3. The circulating fireplace, which consists of a prefabricated steel shell surrounded by masonry. It, too, looks like a conventional fireplace and is a permanent part of the house; but it differs from the other built-ins in that the shell is made of two well-separated layers of steel. Air is admitted into this space through a grilled opening in the base, is heated as it passes up through the space, and is readmitted to the room and sometimes into adjoining rooms through grilled openings above the fireplace. Thus it supplies heat much like a warm-air heating system.

4. The free-standing fireplace, which is a prefabricated steel or cast-iron unit that can be set on the floor anywhere, hung on a wall or suspended from the ceiling. Although connected to a flue (all fireplaces except those which heat by electricity have flues), it is

A built-in prefabricated fireplace costs less than a masonry fireplace, though the cost differential is not too substantial if you build it into a brick wall like this. (Western Fireplaces)

Because conventional and built-in prefabricated fireplaces heat almost entirely by radiation, you must sit in front of them and diagonally to the sides to be warm. This long, low masonry fireplace is set flush with a wall covered with ceramic tile. (Tile Council of America)

not a permanent part of the house. You can take it out and move it around as you would a refrigerator.

In addition to fireplaces, there are wood- or coal-burning stoves. In essence, these are the same as free-standing fireplaces, except that most of them are fully enclosed and you cannot see the fire.

Conventional and prefabricated built-in fireplaces heat almost entirely by radiation. This means, that to enjoy the warming effect, you must position the fireplace so that the occupants of the room are exposed to the heat waves, which travel only in straight lines. True, walls and furnishings exposed to the flames also pick up heat from them and this is given off to the air. It is also true that after a fireplace has been in use for a while, the materials surounding the firebox and flue become warm and give off heat. But in both cases, the effect is minimal. To get any real comfort out of fireplaces of this type, you must sit where you can see the fire and the fire can, in effect, see you.

Circulating fireplaces, on the other hand, heat by both radiation and convection. The flames heat by radiation. At the same time, the air passing through the shell of the firebox is heated by convection, and when the air returns to the room it sets up convection currents which raise the temperature of the entire room. As a result, the location of the fireplace is less critical than it is in the case of a conventional or prefabricated built-in fireplace because you get a fair amount of warmth out of it even if you're not sitting in front of it.

Free-standing fireplaces are even better heat sources—provided they are not heavily insulated—for you get radiant heat from the flames and also from the shell when it becomes hot. In addition, air circulating around the shell is heated by convection. So even though you may be to the side or even behind the fireplace, you still get a great deal of comfort from it. (Stoves heat in the same way; but, as noted earlier, the fire is usually completely enclosed so that heat is radiated only from the steel box surrounding the flames.)

From this brief description of how the different types of fireplaces work, it should be clear that if you want a fireplace primarily to supply heat, the first thing you must decide is which type will serve you best. This, in turn, depends to large extent on the layout of the room and also on its decoration and architectural style.

In a compact, more or less square room, a conventional or prefabricated built-in fireplace should be adequate. But in a very large room, a long, narrow room or an irregular room, a circulating fireplace would be more effective. All three types are compatible with any kind of decoration and architecture.

From the heating standpoint, a free-standing fireplace is suitable to all room layouts. But its modern appearance generally limits it to homes of contemporary and modern design or to very informal houses, such as weekend ski lodges.

Should the Fireplace Be Located on an Outside Wall or Within the House?

If you're putting in a prefabricated built-in or a free-standing fireplace, you can ignore this question, because such fireplaces usually do not have masonry chimneys. They are, instead, vented into insulated metal flue pipes, which occupy so little space that you can run them up through rooms, across ceilings and through walls almost at will. Consequently, the fireplaces can be located almost anywhere.

But when you put in a conventional or a circulating fireplace, metal flues are rarely used except in earthquake zones, and the bulk of the masonry chimney above the fireplace must be taken into account. It occupies considerable space. Together with the fireplace, it requires very substantial foundations.

If you are building a new house, there is little to stop you from placing the fireplace and chimney wherever you want. The location is usually determined by the overall design of the house, but sticklers for detail are not content to base their decision on this alone. Outside chimneys—those built against the outside of an exterior wall—have certain advantages and disadvantages. Inside chimneys—those entirely inside the house (including those on the inside of an exterior wall)—also have advantages and disadvantages.

To be specific, outside chimneys don't take up valuable floor space. They usually help to reduce construction costs slightly, not because they themselves are less expensive than inside chimneys, but because they do not complicate the framing of the house. They are relatively easy to flash; consequently, there is less likely to be leakage through the roof around them. Since three sides of the chimney are exposed to air, the chances of flames or fumes working through cracks in the chimney into the house are reduced 75 percent; and repairs to the chimneys are much easier to make. On

Centered in the long wall of a two-story living room, the fireplace and chimney reach up and up. A certain amount of heat escapes through the masonry at all levels.

the other hand, the chimney often detracts from the appearance of the house. This, of course, is quite unnecessary—even inexcusable. Many outside chimneys are handsome and enhance the house. But as a rule, such beauty is attained by increasing the size of the chimney and thus negating its inherent cost advantage.

9

Outside chimneys have always been more common in the South than in the North because the warmer climate precluded the necessity (in Colonial times) of central chimneys. Early builders recognized the architectural importance of these chimneys and gave them tremendous mass as well as great beauty. From the size of the chimney at right you can tell that it served a large kitchen fireplace and a smaller fireplace on the second floor. The main chimney opposite also served fireplaces on two floors. The chimney is corbelled at the top to improve appearance and to shed water better. (Colonial Williamsburg)

By contrast, an inside chimney is a space-waster—even more of a space-waster than you might suspect, because there must be a 2-inch open space between the sides of the chimney and surrounding combustible material. And, too, it may detract from the appearance of a house if the projection above the roof is not well located or given sufficient bulk. On the other hand, as early New Englanders discovered, an inside chimney gives off considerable warmth to the rooms surrounding it; and it's a simple matter to build one chimney that serves two, three or even four fireplaces (this represents an enormous saving over an equivalent number of outside chimneys, each serving only one fireplace). In addition, the cost of installing and operating an oil- or gas-fired heating system can be reduced somewhat if the furnace is centrally located in the house and is vented into a centrally located chimney. Finally, inside chimneys have better draft, because the masonry retains heat better.

If you want to add a conventional or circulating fireplace to an existing house, however, an inside chimney is a poor choice unless the fireplace is located in the center of a one-story area in which the roof serves as the ceiling. In any other location, you must rip out and rebuild a large section of the framing walls and floors.

Where in the Living Room Should the Fireplace Be Located?

The normal location is more or less in the middle of a wall. Other locations are in an inside corner, at the apex of an outside corner, in a peninsula or as an island in the middle of the room.

The island fireplace is usually open on all sides, so it can radiate heat in all directions, but it may be open only on two opposite sides. The most spectacular island fireplace I am familiar with is a huge one in the lobby of the Drake Hotel in Chicago, but there are many others of less pretentious design in modern homes. They are eye-catchers, no question about it. You enter the room and are immediately drawn to them. And they are fun to sit around on a chilly evening. But they don't have quite the effect of a bonfire in the middle of a campfire circle because the big hanging hood required to carry off the smoke interferes—sometimes badly—with the view across the fire, so you feel cut off from the people on the far side. In addition, the fireplace completely dominates the room and makes it difficult to furnish, unless it is so large that the fireplace can be tucked away in one corner, leaving the rest of the area more or less free.

The peninsula fireplace is built into a wall that partially divides

The several possible locations for a fireplace.

A free-standing fireplace in an island position can be enjoyed from all sides. As with all fireplaces of this type, the flue and chimney are prefabricated from metal. The canopy around the top is used for lighting the area. (Goodwin of California)

a large room into two smaller areas. The fireplace can open into either area, but as a rule opens into both. If placed in the end of the wall—as it generally is—it opens in three directions.

All these arrangements are attractive but present two problems:

1. If you cluster furniture around the fireplace in the usual way—with chairs or love seats on both sides and a sofa directly in front of the hearth—it impedes passage from one room area to the other. As a result, you may have to place furniture only on the solid-wall side of the fireplace and across the front—which prevents the coziness most people want in a fireplace furniture grouping.

2. Since people tend to gravitate to a fireplace, the purpose of the peninsula wall—to provide some privacy for the areas it separates—is at least partially destroyed: the people standing around the fireplace at the open end of the wall cannot help seeing what is going on behind the wall. This may not be a serious drawback; but suppose the fireplace is in the end of a peninsula separating the living from the dining area. It's a cold night and people are

This is a cross between an island and peninsula fireplace. Open in front and back, it serves both living room and dining room. (John Fulker)

Outside corner fireplaces can be enjoyed from two sides. One of the virtues of most raised fireplaces is that you can build a fire in them more easily; but the depth of this fireplace negates this advantage. (Bennett-Ireland)

standing around the fireplace. How can the hostess or maid get things on the dining table without being seen? And after dinner is finished, what guest will particularly enjoy standing by the fireplace and watching the mess being cleared away?

The fireplace in an outside corner is somewhat similar. In this case, however, it is located at the end of a wall that makes a right-angle turn and continues. Outside corners are not common in houses, but they are not uncommon either. You find them most often in large rooms with alcoves.

Fireplaces installed in outside corners are open in front and at one end so the flames radiate heat in two directions. Like all multi-opening fireplaces, they excite interest because they are fairly

16

TOP   *Large corner fireplace in the dining room of the Peyton Randolph house in Williamsburg.* (Colonial Williamsburg)

CENTER   *This is an unusual corner fireplace because it is square across the front; but the effect is the same. Because it's raised off the floor, it can be seen better from distant parts of the large room.* (John Fulker)

BOTTOM   *A fireplace set close to a corner but not in the corner cannot heat a very large area and complicates the furnishing of the room; but this fireplace is in a dining room, where such problems are less important. The paneling is old. The device to the left of the fireplace is an antique meat roaster.*

TOP   There's ample space for people to congregate around this magnificent fireplace, which is set in one of the long walls of an enormous room. (John Fulker)

CENTER   This fireplace is in the end wall of the living room, but the room is large enough so a number of people can warm themselves without crowding. The fireplace is new; the beautiful mantel and paneling were taken from an early New York State home.

BOTTOM   This is not exactly an ideal location for a fireplace since there's a passageway between it and the seating area; but sometimes such things cannot be avoided. (John Fulker)

unusual. But like the fireplaces already discussed, they complicate furniture arrangement, and this is likely, in turn, to complicate the use of the room.

Inside-corner fireplaces are a much older idea. They were apparently first used in the United States by the Swedes who settled Delaware about 1640. But no one today knows why.

The best reason for an inside-corner fireplace is that, no matter where you sit in the room, you can see the flames and, if you're not in the opposite corner, soak up some of the heat from them. But if you put a sofa directly in front of the fireplace, it messes up the furniture arrangement in the rest of the room. More important, the fireplace takes up considerable floor space.

So we come at last to the favorite location for fireplaces—in the middle of a wall.

Given a room that is more or less square, it doesn't make any difference whether the fireplace is in one of the end walls or one of the side walls. But in long, narrow rooms, placement in a side wall is preferred. One reason for this is a universal quirk of human nature that too few home owners take into account. As I said before, people naturally gravitate to a fireplace. So if your fireplace is built into the narrow end wall of your living room, everybody at a party crowds uncomfortably around it, leaving the opposite end of the room unpopulated. On the other hand, if the fireplace is in the long side wall of the room, there is more space for people to stand around it and less space in the room is wasted.

The other advantage of a side-wall fireplace in a long, narrow room is that there isn't space to put a sofa close in front of it. This, of course, means you can't have a cozy, U-shaped furniture grouping around it, and that may bother you. On the other hand, it greatly improves the furniture arangement in the entire room. It also improves the traffic pattern through the room.

Where Should a Fireplace Be Located in Other Rooms?

Fireplaces in dining rooms, family rooms used only by the family, studies, bedrooms, kitchens—yes, and why not those huge bathrooms so many people are building these days?—are another breed of cat. The arguments concerning the placement of fireplaces in living rooms are not so applicable.

For example, a fireplace in the end wall of a long, narrow dining room is much more desirable than one in the side wall. An inside corner fireplace in a den or kitchen is a delight. An outside corner or peninsula fireplace in a bedroom works out well because the smaller area into which it opens can be used as a dressing room or reading nook.

Should the Fireplace Be Flush with, or Projecting from, the Wall?

This may, perhaps, seem like a small point, but it's one I feel strongly about, because I've lived with several fireplaces that stuck out from the wall and I was never very happy with them.

To begin with, such a fireplace takes up floor space.

If the fireplace projects more than about a foot, it creates unattractive nooks on either side that are hard to furnish and that

LEFT   *This fireplace projects about 9 inches from the wall. It is the focal point of a well-balanced composition that was simpler to create than you might suspect. The paneled wall effect was achieved by applying moldings to a flat plaster surface.*
RIGHT   *By itself, this flush-with-the-wall fireplace would not be particularly distinguished; but it invariably invites exclamations of pleasure because of the way it is combined with the built-in lighted cupboards.*

are more or less useless since nobody seems to want to sit in them. The best way to handle the nooks—if you can afford to give up the floor space—is to fill them in with bookcases or cabinets.

And the fireplace itself is too often unattractive, especially if the wall above it does not project, too. It has the general look of a wart.

I am, of course, talking in terms of the ideal fireplace. There are many situations in which the projection of a fireplace from a wall almost cannot be avoided. This is particularly true when you're adding a fireplace *within* an existing house. And if you're putting in a free-standing fireplace, projection is unavoidable.

But in any other circumstance, try your best to push the fireplace back into the wall so only the mantel shelf projects.

20

RIGHT *Museum directors have rated this mid-eighteenth-century paneled wall one of the most perfect—if not the most perfect— in America; and the fireplace rates right along with it.*
BELOW *An almost identical fireplace in the same house. The heavy molding follows the arch of the lintel and would not be permitted in today's homes because it might be ignited by a roaring fire. Nevertheless, it has survived for over 200 years.*

Should the Fireplace Have a Raised Hearth?

In the past, the elevated fireplace was virtually unknown. It has become common only within the past twenty-five years. The reasons for this are not very clear—at least to me. In his little book *The Forgotten Art of Building a Good Fireplace*,* Vrest Orton suggests that modern fireplaces are raised because they're so small—unnecessarily small—that this is the only way people can really see the flames and feel the warmth. This is probably as good an explanation as any.

More practical reasons for elevating fireplaces are that (1) the fires are easier to lay and tend because you don't have to stoop down so far (this is especially important in the case of a very small fireplace; on the other hand, in order to reach all the way into the fireplace you may have to climb up on the forehearth, thus negating the less-stooping advantage); (2) you can use the forehearth as a bench to sit on and place potted plants on; (3) island fireplaces almost have to be raised if people sitting around them are to be able to see past overhanging hoods; (4) in a bedroom a small raised fireplace does a better job of warming the entire body as you finish drying off after a bath.

* Dublin, N. H.: Yankee, 1969.

LEFT   *A great stone fireplace at the end of a long living-dining area is raised well off the floor so it can be enjoyed from the opposite end of the room.* (Moore, Grover, Harper, architects)
RIGHT   *A very modern fireplace with a partially cantilevered forehearth that is surfaced with ceramic tile.* (John Fulker)

But none of these arguments explains the really widespread use of raised fireplaces today. (A year ago when I was inspecting houses for sale in Memphis, I was flabbergasted to discover that in practically every house the fireplaces were elevated.)

I guess I am more of a traditionalist than I think, but I simply do not feel that a raised fireplace is more functional than one level with the floor; and it certainly is no more attractive. On the contrary, there probably isn't more than one attractive raised fireplace for every ten attractive floor units. I can't find any clear reason for this either, except possibly for the fact that the forehearth—which is the least attractive part of a fireplace—is too dominant.

Of course, these are personal opinions. You may prefer raised fireplaces, and if so, there's no reason for not building one. But do at least give extra-careful thought to their design.

How Will the Fireplace Area Be Furnished?

Given the opportunity, most home owners like to place an over-stuffed chair or love seat on either side of the fireplace at right angles to the opening, and a sofa facing it. But this arrangement very often does not work well because (1) it cuts the fireplace off from the rest of the room; (2) it prevents many of the people at a party from getting as close to the fireplace as they would like;

(3) it takes up a great deal of space; (4) it sometimes interferes with traffic passing through the room; and (5) it is very hard to light the area so that people on the sofa can read or sew.

Actually, this arrangement is generally suited only to very large rooms or long, narrow rooms with the fireplace at one end. In most other rooms, the sofa should be eliminated. And in some cases, one or both of the side chairs or love seats can be eliminated, too.

A fireplace does influence furniture arrangement, but it should definitely not distort it. Since you use the entire room, not just the area around the fireplace, your first thought must be to arrange the furniture to suit the room. Only then should you worry about the fireplace-area arrangement.

When working on the latter, the following details should be observed:

1. The chairs or love seats at the sides of the fireplace should be set back roughly two feet from the fireplace opening. One reason for this is to avoid obscuring the mantel. The other is to protect the furniture fabrics and woods from debilitating exposure to the flames.

2. The sofa across the front of the fireplace should be at least six feet from the opening, to allow for movement in the immediate area of the fireplace and also to protect the piece from intense heat.

What Should the Style of the Fireplace Be?

Semantics don't ordinarily interest me, but at this point I think it's wise to pin down exactly what a fireplace is.

Strictly speaking, it is nothing more than an open-sided box in which a fire is burned. The proportions of the box vary. The opening is usually rectangular but is sometimes arch-shaped, round, half-round or even hexagonal. But in no case does a built-in fireplace

With a brick or marble surround, this would be a pleasant fireplace but not outstanding. The hand-painted tiles make it a charmer.

RIGHT *This large Georgian fireplace fits beautifully in a modern home. To make the white marble mantel, which came from England, stand out from the white wall, architect Jonathan Isleib left a half-inch gap around the edges and painted it black.* (Charles N. Pratt)

BELOW *The fireplace is faced with white Indiana limestone surrounded by a heavy, handsome molding. The large model of a ship's hull serves as the mantel shelf.*

RIGHT   Architects Moore, Grover, and Harper thought this exceptionally wide fireplace required an unusual mantel shelf. They pieced three Mexican ceramic flower boxes together end to end and supported them on a pair of round concrete posts. The overmantel piece is a Mexican candelabrum.

BELOW   This is a brand-new fireplace in a very modern home. The fireplace itself is flush with the wall but the old mantel, made of rich red marble and imported from France, projects about 6 inches. The forehearth is made of new matching marble. (Jonathan Isleib, architect)

RIGHT *The rough concrete mantel (matching the texture of the raised forehearth) was cast with concave grooves alternating here and there at precise intervals with deep pockets. Instead of screening the entire opening and thus spoiling its lines to some extent, the owners surround the fire alone with a hood-type screen.* (John Fulker)

BELOW *Simple mantel shelf made of a large, rough-sawn timber.*

have any style. Only free-standing fireplaces have a style—usually modern.

What gives a built-in fireplace style is the way the vertical surface surrounding the opening is treated. In many cases, this is simply an unadorned wall of brick, stone, wood, etc. If the wall is of noncombustible material, the fireplace opening is usually flush with it. If the wall is combustible, the fireplace opening is surrounded with a strip of noncombustible material about six inches wide, which is recessed about an inch behind the wall.

The fireplace has a mantel and perhaps a mantel shelf. In this book, a mantel—often called a mantelpiece—is considered to be the ornamental covering around and above the fireplace. The mantel shelf is a shelf directly above the fireplace. Some fireplaces have a mantel without a shelf; others have a shelf without a mantel; others have both.

Whatever the treatment of the wall around a fireplace, it is the mantel that determines whether the fireplace is colonial, French provincial, modern, etc. The treatment, in turn, depends on the architectural style of the house. The two should be in keeping, although this doesn't mean they must be identical in style. For example, the fireplace pictured on page 25 is Georgian, whereas the house is modern; yet the two are completely compatible because one of the pleasant peculiarities of many types of modern architecture is that they gracefully accept some completely different styles of furnishings. But to stick, say, an Italianate fireplace in a New England colonial house would be disconcerting.

Having made this point, let me backtrack a minute and branch off in a slightly different direction.

Just as the mantel or wall treatment sets the style of the fireplace, it also determines whether the fireplace is beautiful, ugly or just sort of blah. True, the facing of the fireplace—the covering on the exposed edges—contributes to the feeling the fireplace evokes when you look at it; but it is of secondary importance.

You can test this statement by taking three pieces of paper and placing them around the edges of any of the fireplaces illustrated on these pages. You will find that when the wall area around any fireplace is blanked out, the fireplace doesn't have very much interest or appeal. One rectangular fireplace is almost identical to another.

A fireplace to be beautiful—and who wants one that isn't beautiful?—is strictly dependent on its surrounding wall. A fire burning on the hearth may make it a little more beautiful (or a little less ugly), but it's wrong to count on a fire to make a silk purse out of a sow's ear, because you don't have a fire every day of the year. A fireplace should be beautiful without a fire, and that is possible only if the surrounding wall is beautiful.

Millions of home owners have hideous or nondescript fireplaces that could be made beautiful if the mantel and/or mantel shelf were torn off and replaced. And other millions would greatly improve fireplaces that are inherently attractive if they would redecorate the wall on either side of the mantel.

What Will the Fireplace Cost? To get to more practical matters, the cost of the fireplace must be considered carefully before you build one. Unfortunately, there are no accurate average figures to serve as a guide. But here's a rough idea of the expenditure you can expect to make:

- CONVENTIONAL MASONRY FIREPLACE $1500 in a new house; $1800 in an existing house if the fireplace is on an outside wall; $2500 if within the house

- CIRCULATING FIREPLACE About the same prices

- PREFABRICATED BUILT-IN FIREPLACE $800

- FREE-STANDING FIREPLACE $400

Of course, the only sensible way to price conventional and circulating fireplaces is to give a mason a picture or, better, a plan of the fireplace and ask him to make a firsthand study of the problems involved in installing it in the selected location. You may also need a carpenter to study and give a price on the work involved in framing around the fireplace. Since the project is expensive, ask two or three masons—and carpenters—for estimates.

A pretty accurate idea of the cost of installing a prefabricated built-in or a free-standing fireplace can usually be had from the dealer from whom you buy the unit. The figure will, of course, be higher if you have a carpenter make the installation (you don't need a mason) than if you make it yourself (a relatively simple undertaking).

29

How Will You Provide Ventilation for the Fire?

Fires need air to burn. Probably the principal reason so many fireplaces give off little heat and lots of smoke is that they have an insufficient air supply.

In days gone by, when no one worried much about insulating houses, weatherstripping doors and windows, and using vapor barriers to prevent condensation of moisture in the exterior walls and roof, more than enough air entered the house through tiny openings to keep fires burning briskly. But today most new houses and many renovated old houses are so tightly constructed that natural air infiltration is severely restricted—and what might otherwise be an excellent fireplace proves to be a constant annoyance.

It's all well and good to say, "Well, if my fireplace smokes, I can always open a window to give it the air it needs." But opening windows not only negates the heating function of a fireplace but also causes your heating plant to work harder. So this can hardly be called an intelligent answer to the problem. A far better approach is to make special provision for introducing the necessary air. This, of course, is much easier to do when you're building a fireplace than as an afterthought.

For a conventional masonry fireplace or circulating fireplace— both of which require substantial foundations—the easiest thing to do is to install an ash dump in the hearth and a perforated ventilating brick which opens into the dump in the fireplace foundation wall. (Naturally, this presupposes that you have a basement or crawl space.) Basement air flows through the ventilating brick into the ash dump; and if you keep the door at the top of the dump cracked open, the air flows directly into the fireplace.

If a house is built on a concrete slab, the ash dump is only about a foot deep and contains a bucket that is lifted out through the top when full of ashes. The dump can be used for ventilation, however, if you make the hole somewhat larger than the bucket and bring outdoor air into it through a three- or four-inch duct.

Fireplaces without ash dumps are ventilated in similar fashion. Air is brought in through an under-floor duct connected to a small hole made in the hearth just in front of the fire. An ash-dump door mounted in the hole controls the amount of incoming air.

Handle prefabricated built-in fireplaces in the same way. If the air opening cannot be installed in the hearth, put it in the fore-hearth. A similar approach must be used for free-standing fireplaces

Ventilation for this fireplace is provided by an underfloor duct leading to a small heating register set in the forehearth.

that have a hearth laid on the floor. But for off-the-floor free-standing fireplaces, the only thing left you can do is to put the air inlet opening in the floor as close to the fireplace opening as possible.

Can a New Fireplace Be Connected into an Existing Chimney?

The answer to this question is a resounding no. Every fireplace; every stove; every gas-, oil- or coal-fired heating plant; every gas-, oil- or coal-fired water heater; and every gas-, oil- or coal-fired cook stove should have its own flue.

This may come as a surprise if you're familiar with old houses, because in these one flue often serves two or even three fireplaces or stoves. But for once the old-timers were wrong. When there are several openings in a flue, gas and sparks may pass from one to the other. In addition, operation of the fireplaces or stoves may be affected.

Of course, if you have a chimney with a flue that is no longer being used, you can vent a new fireplace into this. But in all other cases, you must build a new chimney or add a new flue to an existing chimney (which amounts to building a new chimney because you must add a new flue surrounded by bricks to one side of the present chimney).

Who Should Design Your New Fireplace?

Both architects and masons are competent to design fireplaces and chimneys, though there is considerable professional jealousy between them. Architects feel that masons know little about fireplace construction and masons return this feeling about architects. Both may be right to some extent, because there are plenty of poor fire-

Only an architect (in this case, the firm of Moore, Grover, Harper) would think of developing a fireplace like this. It is set at an angle to the room at right; behind it is a stairway. To emphasize its unusual position, a triangular mirror was mounted on the wall above it.

places in each camp. That's something you should try to find out before you hire either one: What is the man's reputation for designing fireplaces that work well?

That, however, is somewhat beside the point. Although fireplace design seems complicated to the amateur, the principles are so well established that any experienced architect or mason should be able to draw plans for a good one. You can probably draw perfectly good plans yourself. The advantage an architect enjoys is that he is also trained and capable of designing the fireplace wall so you have a beautiful installation. Very few masons have comparable ability.

It follows that, if you're putting in a conventional masonry fireplace, you ought to hire an architect to design it for you. You may also want an architect, if you're putting in a circulating or prefabricated built-in fireplace, to design the surrounding wall, mantel, etc.

On the other hand, if you trust yourself to design a handsome fireplace wall, there is no need to pay an architect a fee to design the fireplace, because a mason can do this just as well—and without a design fee.

2 Masonry Fireplaces

In his time, man has built fireplaces in just about every conceivable shape, in an enormous range of sizes and even of a considerable number of materials, including wood, which was the standard material for building chimneys for many, many years. Undoubtedly, as the years roll on, other designs not yet thought of will be attempted. But for the moment the conventional masonry fireplace is pretty well standardized because, when properly designed and built, it works very well and looks attractive. For this we can give thanks mainly to an eighteenth-century genius best known as Count Rumford, though he was actually named Benjamin Thompson and was born in Woburn, Massachusetts. Rumford developed the rules for shaping the fireplace to produce the most warmth.

Masonry fireplaces are the standard by which all other types of fireplace are judged. Despite their two serious drawbacks—high cost and relatively poor heating performance—they outnumber all

LEFT *An enormous brick fireplace and chimney in the two-story living room of a remodeled barn. The right side of the fireplace is angled to parallel the side of the chimney. The raised forehearth is a favorite sitting place at parties.*

RIGHT *For his own home, architect Jonathan Isleib raised the fireplace off the floor and surrounded it on all four sides with black slate projecting 4 inches from the wall. The forehearth was omitted on the theory that it wasn't needed because the fireplace is deeper than most and has a roll-down screen which completely seals the opening.*

the other types combined. The main reason can only be that, in the public mind, they have a certain cachet.

A friend of mine was telling me a year ago about the success one of his sons was having in the building business even in the depths of the latest recession. The young man, new to the business, was putting up low-cost homes in Massachusetts. In passing, I asked his father what kind of fireplace he was putting in. I assumed that they must be prefabs because of their lower cost.

But no. "Oh, he's building regular brick fireplaces," the father answered.

"But why?"

"He figures it's the kind most home buyers want. And he must be right if the number of people placing orders for his houses means anything."

Well, you say, that's in Massachusetts. But it is equally true in most other states. The masonry fireplace is a known quantity. Reliable (well, we all hope so, anyway) and durable. It's a permanent part of the house. It increases property values. Other than the free-standing fireplace, it is the only type which can be built in countless different shapes.

Building Masonry Fireplaces

Even though you can design a masonry fireplace (if you use a fireplace-building manual as your guide), you should not try to build one unless you have had a great deal of experience building masonry walls. There simply are too many opportunities for going wrong. For instance, if the chimney leans, it may fall. If the joints are not properly filled, flames may escape and start a fire in the structure of the house. If you deviate from the blueprints a little, the fireplace may smoke so badly that you'll have to have it rebuilt.

But just because you're not a fireplace builder doesn't mean you shouldn't know how one should be built. Such knowledge not only enables you to check on what your architect and/or mason have concocted but also will help you to cope with the fireplace if it turns out to be cantankerous. Besides, what good is a book about fireplaces if it doesn't explain them?

In a round house, a round fireplace. Unfortunately, because of the shape of the firebox, the walls do not reflect as much heat into the house as a firebox of conventional shape (the side and front walls reflect heat back into the firebox). (John Fulker)

ABOVE This was once a screened porch. When the owners enclosed it, they built this dramatic fieldstone wall and installed a 4-foot-diameter circular fireplace in the center. The firebox is of conventional shape.

RIGHT The lines of the fireplace follow the lines of the roof, and the square chimney is set on the diagonal to carry out the angular theme. Both are made of brick.
(John Fulker)

ABOVE   As in many fireplaces
with unusual-shaped openings,
the firebox here is of conventional
design; only the breast is arched.
(John Fulker)
RIGHT   As contrasted to the round
fireplace, the walls of this gigantic
fireplace reflect maximum heat
into the room. (John Fulker)

FOUNDATION   Because a single fireplace and chimney often exceed ten tons, the importance of a firm foundation under them is obvious. In old New England houses, it is quite common to find foundations that measure ten feet square.

Code requirements vary, of course (as they do for all parts of a fireplace). But generally the base of the foundation—the footing— is an 8- to 12-inch-thick slab of poured reinforced concrete that extends at least 6 inches beyond all sides of the structure it supports. The bottom of the slab must be laid below the frost line, or at least a foot below grade level in frost-free areas.

In a basementless house built on a slab, the fireplace normally rests directly on the footing. In a house with a basement or crawl space, foundation walls are built up from the footing to the hearth. These can be made of poured concrete, concrete block or brick. They should be a minimum of 8 inches thick in a one-story house; 12 inches in a two-story house.

ASH PIT   The ash pit is an opening under the hearth, within the foundations, into which ashes are swept for easy collection. Relatively few fireplaces have one, but it's a convenience feature you should certainly consider. It adds little to the cost of a fireplace.

In a house with a basement, the ash pit is the hollow space within the foundation walls. At the top, in the floor of the hearth, is a small metal door, called an ash dump, which pivots upward so you can sweep the ashes into the pit. In the side of one of the foundation walls, at the bottom of the pit, is a metal clean-out door through which the ashes are removed.

In a slab house, ash pits are less common but can easily be incorporated by making a hole in the concrete footing under the hearth. This is covered with an ash dump. A pail is put in the hole for collecting and carting away the ashes.

A second advantage of an ash pit is that outside air can be introduced through it to provide ample oxygen for the fire. The air is brought in through a ventilating brick or duct as described in Chapter 1.

HEARTH   The flat surface on which a fire is laid is actually in two parts, though they may be made of one material. The part within the fireplace is the hearth proper. The part projecting into the room is the forehearth.

The hearth is usually made of firebrick—a refractory ceramic brick that resists high heat—but is sometimes made of stone

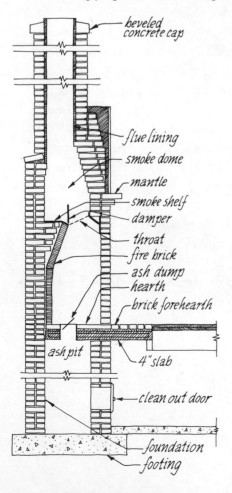

Drawing showing the parts of a masonry fireplace and chimney.

beveled concrete cap

flue lining

smoke dome

mantle

smoke shelf

damper

throat

fire brick

ash dump

hearth

brick forehearth

ash pit

4" slab

clean out door

foundation

footing

RIGHT *A sleek modern fireplace with a cantilevered forehearth. The wall on either side of the fireplace opening is faced with mosaic tiles. Above are large slabs of travertine.* (John Fulker)

OPPOSITE *Here the raised forehearth rests on the floor, which is laid on a concrete slab; but in a house with a basement, it would rest on the foundations for the fireplace. Although this is a masonry fireplace, it has a prefabricated metal chimney, visible through the clerestory window.* (Tile Council of America)

(generally less satisfactory because it is too rough to sweep properly). In a slab house, the firebrick is laid directly on the foundation. But if there is a deep ash pit in the foundation, the firebrick is laid on a reinforced concrete slab covering the pit; or the sides of the ash pit are corbelled in toward the opening just below the ash dump, and the firebrick is laid on the foundation.

The forehearth is, in effect, hung on the side of the foundation at the level of the hearth. Since it does not rest on the floor joists, an opening must be framed in the floor for it. The forehearth is then constructed in three ways:

1. It can be supported on a brick arch extending from the front wall of the foundation to a ledger strip nailed to the side of the double header framing the floor opening.

2. It can be supported on a reinforced concrete slab cantilevered from the foundation to a ledger strip.

40

3. It can be supported on long, T-shaped steel strips (T irons) extending from the foundation to a ledger strip. Bricks are laid on edge in mortar between the T irons.

In all three cases, the forehearth is surfaced with brick (not necessarily firebrick), stone, marble, ceramic tile or smooth, colored concrete. The entire structure must be at least 6 inches thick.

If a fireplace is raised off the floor, the hearth is constructed in the same way. As a rule, the forehearth also rests on the foundation, which is enlarged to support it. In a few cases, however, the forehearth is made of a big, thick slab of stone which is cantilevered out from the foundation.

Whatever the construction of the forehearth, it must project at least 16 inches from the face of the fireplace and extend at least 8 inches to either side. For fireplaces with openings exceeding 6 square feet in area, these dimensions must be increased to 20 and

12 inches respectively. If the forehearth is any smaller, there is danger that flying embers will sail right over it, land on the floor or carpet and start a fire.

FIREBOX Sometimes the area in which the fire is actually built is called a combustion chamber. "Firebox" is simpler, though it may mislead people who tend to think of boxes as perfect cubes.

The firebox is anything but a perfect cube. For that, major credit goes to Count Rumford, who discovered that, for a fireplace to radiate the maximum amount of heat into a room, the sides should not be vertical and at right angles to one another.

The back wall of the firebox is much narrower than the front opening. This means that the sides—sometimes called the cheeks— slant in toward the back, thus forming a box which looks like a truncated V rather than a rectangle.

The sides are straight up and down. The back, on the other hand, is straight to a height of only about 15 inches above the hearth. It then slants or curves gently forward in order to direct more heat into the room and at the same time lead the smoke up into the chimney. (Fireplace dimensions are discussed on page 62.)

The firebox is generally lined with 2-inch-thick firebrick laid in a special heat-resistant mortar known as fireclay. The joints should

RIGHT *A brand new fireplace built to Count Rumford's specifications. The height is 5 inches greater than the width.*
OPPOSITE *A new fireplace built to the design and dimensions of an early Colonial fireplace. As in most early-day fireplaces, the lintel is an oak timber.* (Jackson Hand)

be only ¼ inch thick. Behind the lining, common bricks are used. The total thickness of the walls should be no less than 8 inches.

If a firebrick lining is omitted, wall thickness must be increased to at least 12 inches.

A 4-inch air space must be provided between the back of a fireplace and all woodwork.

LINTEL   The lintel forms the top of the fireplace opening and supports the masonry above it. In the old days it was often a large oak timber. Many of these have survived, even though charred, because our ancestors built much larger and higher fireplaces than we do today. In other old fireplaces, as well as in some modern ones, the lintel is a long cut stone. In most current fireplaces, however, a wide half-inch-thick strap of iron is used.

Lintels are required only in rectangular fireplace openings. If the opening is arched, bricks set on edge, with a keystone in the middle of the arch, are sufficient to bear the weight of the masonry above. However, care must be taken to make the jambs on which the arch rests heavy enough to resist the thrust of the arch.

JAMBS   The jambs of a fireplace are the exposed edges of the sides. Their width may exceed the thickness of the sides. They are left unfinished or faced with marble, tile or any other ornamental noncombustible material.

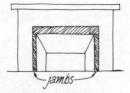

The jambs of the fireplace and area above the lintel constitute the fireplace surround.

In fireplaces with iron lintels, the jambs are finished to match the exposed area directly above the lintel. The three sections constitute the *surround*.

THROAT   The throat is the narrow opening connecting the firebox to the flue. It is at least 6 inches—preferably 8—above the bottom of the lintel.

The width of the throat equals the width of the fireplace opening. But it is only a few inches deep, front to back. In area it should be at least equal to the area of the flue.

DAMPER   Early fireplaces didn't have dampers, and some are built without them today. (This is especially true in summer vacation homes.) But in a year-round dwelling, at a time when energy conservation is of paramount importance, a damper is a must because it enables you to close off the flue when the fireplace is not in use and thus prevent the loss of enormous volumes of room heat up the chimney. It also keeps cold air, dirt, insects and birds out of the room. And because you can adjust it to various partially open positions, it gives you greater control of the draft.

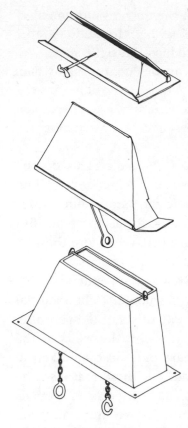

The three types of damper. That in the middle is the most commonly used. High-dome type at bottom is mainly used in multiopening fireplaces.

A damper consists of a cast-iron frame with a cast-iron door pivoted so it swings open toward the smoke shelf. Installed in the throat, with the back edge resting on and cemented to the smoke shelf, the damper should be as wide as the fireplace opening. Its open area should equal at least 90 percent of the flue area.

The damper is controlled either by a lever, chain or a turnscrew that extends through the breast of the fireplace. The lever control (generally called a poker control) is most common because it is simple and inexpensive. It is made with an eye in the end so you can hook it with a poker or tongs to open and close it. With age, however, the lever and damper door tend to become arthritic so that you often have to get down on your knees and manipulate the lever by hand.

The screw-type rotary control is easier to operate, though slower. It, too, can become balky after a time. The chain control can be operated only by reaching into the fireplace.

Dampers are prefabricated in several styles and a considerable number of sizes. Instead of being flat frames that are simply set in the throat, the majority of those used today are more or less pyramidal or square-dome-shaped to serve as forms for the surounding masonry. Thus they simplify construction of the fireplace and reduce cost to a slight extent. But they must be closely coordinated to the size and shape of the fireplaces in which they're used. If you want a very unusual fireplace, you won't necessarily find a prefabricated damper that will work with it; you must either change the fireplace design to suit the dampers available or have one made to order.

SMOKE SHELF   The smoke shelf is behind the throat and directly under the flue. Its job is to stop air flowing down the chimney from reaching the fire and to deflect the air back up the chimney. It is as wide as the throat and from 6 to 12 inches deep, depending on the depth of the firebox.

As a rule, the smoke shelf is a flat ledge, but a concave design is somewhat more efficient in directing downdrafts upward.

SMOKE CHAMBER   Also called the smoke dome, the smoke chamber is a transition area between the fireplace and flue. Here the smoke rising through the throat and damper is gathered in and funneled into the flue.

If the chamber is constructed entirely of masonry, the sloping front and sides must be covered with smoothly troweled cement mortar so that nothing can interfere with the upward movement of the smoke. The alternative is to install a "high-formed" damper with high sides and front designed to produce the right slope.

FLUE   The size of the chimney opening, or flue, through which smoke and gases are carried off to the air is determined by the size of the fireplace and the height of the chimney (see discussion on page 65). But there are certain rules about constructing the flue from which you must not deviate.

First, the flue should be as straight as possible. This doesn't mean that bends are not permissible, because when several fireplaces or heating appliances are vented into the same chimney, it's almost impossible to make all the flues as straight as an arrow. But whatever bends are necessary must be gradual—no more than 30 degrees from the vertical—and the flue liner sections must be mitered so there is no reduction in flue area at the bends.

Second, the flue must be lined with a smooth, tight material that is resistant to high heat and rapid fluctuations in temperature. Refractory bricks can be used; but in that event, the walls of the chimney must be 8 inches thick. Great care must also be taken to make the mortar joints smooth and sound. For these reasons, it is safer and more economical to use liner made of fireclay in sections up to 3 feet long. The minimum thickness is ⅝ inch; and you need only a 4-inch thickness of common brick on the outside. (If the chimney is built of irregular stones, on the other hand, the walls surrounding the liner must be 12 inches thick.)

The flue liner must be solidly supported at the base. Each section is then installed before the chimney is built up around it. The joints between the liner sections must be airtight and struck off smooth on the inside. For mortar, you can use fireclay, or Type M mortar made of 1 part Portland cement, ¼ part hydrated lime and 3 to 3¾ parts sand, or Type S mortar made of 1 part Portland cement, ¼ to ½ part hydrated lime and 3¼ to 4½ parts sand.

The top of the flue lining should project at least 4 inches above the top of the chimney. When there are two or more flues in a chimney, they are cut off at different heights to discourage smoke coming out of one from pouring down another.

The flue is not cemented to the chimney except as necessary to hold it in place. If there are two flues in the same chimney, the liners can be placed against one another but not cemented. However, the joints must be staggered at least 7 inches. If there are more than two flues, they can be grouped in twos; but each pair must be separated from another pair or from a single flue by a withe (masonry partition) at least 4 inches thick.

CHIMNEY   As noted above, the walls of a chimney with fireclay flue lining need be only 4 inches thick if constructed of brick (or solid concrete blocks or reinforced concrete) but must be at least 12 inches thick if constructed of rubble (uncut) stone. They may, of course, be much thicker; and in many cases they should be to improve the appearance of the chimney.

Skinny chimneys, whether exposed on an outside wall or projecting above the middle of a roof, are rarely attractive, because they are out of scale with the house. And for this reason they call attention to themselves and thus, in effect, accentuate their ugliness. There is absolutely no excuse for this. The chimney is a very important architectural element of a house, and it should therefore be handsome—as old fireplace builders, particularly in the South, knew.

Some years ago, when I was building a large New England colonial house for sale, I took exception to the chimney the architect had designed. For one thing, it was not in the exact middle of the roof. This was unavoidable because of the size and plan of the house; nevertheless, the chimney looked too much off center, yet it wasn't far enough off center to give the house asymmetrical balance. The other problem—which aggravated the first—was that the chimney was too small. When I asked the architect to correct matters, his first suggestion was to install a second fake chimney to balance the real one. But I would have no part of such phoniness. So he went back to his drawing board and returned with a plan to increase the bulk of the chimney.

Not knowing very much about chimney construction at that time, I objected on the ground that this would take too much space out of the center of the house. "Not at all," he answered. "We'll corbel the chimney. When we get up into the attic, we'll offset the bricks outward. All the increased bulk will be built in the attic and above the roof."

And that's what we ended up doing. The chimney is still off center on the roof, but because of its size, I doubt that many people are conscious of this. I am certain that few, if any, think it detracts from the appearance of the house.

There is one other reason for increasing the wall thickness of

Compare the chimneys on these houses. The house at top is small and charming with its gingerbread, but the chimney is entirely too little—a pipestem. The house below is large and imposing and the chimney is in perfect scale.

BELOW   Chimney corbelled below the roof to give it greater mass above the roof. The bricks in each succeeding higher course are set a bit further out. The result is an inverted stairway arrangement.

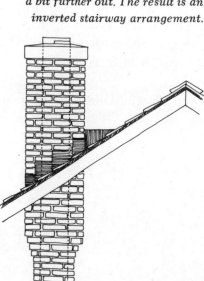

This is the house I built. Below the roof, the chimney is about half this size. I asked my architect to increase its mass so its off-center location would not be so disturbing.

an inside chimney where it projects above the roof, and it's a very practical one. During gales, chimney tops may sway and open up the mortar joints at the roof line. This allows sparks from the flue to escape and set fire to the roof. To help prevent this, it is advisable to increase the thickness of the upper part of the chimney to at least 8 inches. The increased thickness extends from just below the roof to the chimney top.

Whatever the thickness of chimney walls, all wood beams, joists, headers, studs and furring strips must be separated from the outside walls of the chimney by a 2-inch air space (however, the ends of girders may be supported by the chimney if there is at least 8 inches of solid masonry between them and the flue liner). To prevent flames from roaring up through the space, the space must be firestopped at each floor level with asbestos-board or other noncombustible material.

On the other hand, exterior chimneys can be set against the sheathing; and subfloors can be placed within ¾ inch of interior chimneys.

To improve draft, the top of a chimney must be at least 3 feet

RIGHT This is a house of many angles, and the massive chimney is angled accordingly. It is covered with white cement plaster.

BELOW These are the chimneys for the two fireplaces on page 168. Surfaced with concrete plaster, they are far bigger than the flues running through them but are in perfect proportion to the house. Imagine the effect if they were smaller.

RIGHT *Here the large chimney is the same shape and size as the fireplace area. (Tile Council of America)*

BELOW *This diagram helps to clarify the rules about extending a chimney above the roof.*

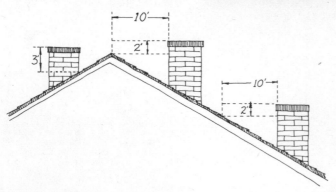

above the highest point at which the chimney emerges from the roof. In addition, the top must be at least 2 feet above any part of any building within 10 feet. What this means is that, unless your roof is almost flat or unless the chimney is placed very close to the high point of the roof, the chimney may have to extend more than 3 feet above the roof. For example, suppose that the upper side of your chimney is 9 feet 11 inches below the roof ridge (measured horizontally). If the roof has only a 1-inch pitch, the chimney need be only 3 feet high. But if the pitch is 2 inches, the chimney should be 3 feet 8 inches high. If the pitch is 4 inches, the chimney should be 5 feet 4 inches high. If the pitch is 6 inches, the chimney should be 7 feet high.

The same situation (but not necessarily the same figures) applies if the chimney is more than 10 feet from the roof ridge but less than 10 feet from the side of a pitched roof; or if it is less than 10 feet from a dormer; or less than 10 feet from a cupola; or less than 10 feet from a barn, neighbor's house or apartment building.

Also to improve draft, the top of the chimney should be capped with a 2-inch or greater thickness of cement mortar which slopes from the four sides of the chimney up toward the flue liner. This not only directs air currents upward over the flue but also allows water to drain off rapidly. Ideally, the cap (and usually the top courses of brick just below it) should overhang the sides of the

52

chimney an inch or two so the drip water will fall clear of the chimney.

If clay chimney pots are installed above the flues, they must have the same area as the flues.

A spark arrester is advisable—and may be required—if you live in a wooded area. Made of rust-resistant mesh with openings not less than $\frac{5}{16}$ inch or more than $\frac{5}{8}$ inch across, it should have a gross open area at least twice the net flue area. For all practical purposes, this means that the top of the arrester (which can be made of mesh or solid metal) must be at least one foot above the chimney cap. The arrester must, of course, be securely anchored to the cap.

To prevent water from leaking through the roof around the sides of the chimney, the chimney must be well flashed with corrosion-resistant metal—preferably copper because of its long life and resistance to the alkalis in mortar.

Flashing a chimney is a job for experts. First, strips of metal are placed around the sides of the chimney and bent flat over the roof. The roofing is laid over these except on the down-slope side. Then additional strips of metal which overhang the vertical sides of the first strips are set into the mortar joints in the chimney to form an apron. Finally, the mortar joints are filled with caulking compound.

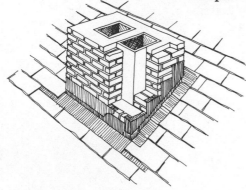

How a central chimney is flashed.

On chimneys placed well below the roof ridge, additional water protection may be provided by constructing a tent-shaped cricket, or saddle, behind the up-slope side of the chimney. This is designed to divert the water flowing down the roof around the sides of the chimney.

Upon completion of a fireplace and chimney, before they have been enclosed, each flue should be tested by building a strong, smoky fire in the fireplace. After this is going well, cover the outlet of the flue at the top of the chimney with a wet blanket and look for smoke escaping through cracks in the masonry to the surrounding air or into adjoining flues. Any that you find must be sealed before the fireplace is used.

Protecting Against Earthquakes

In areas subject to earthquakes, fireplaces and chimneys must be reinforced from top to bottom with four rows of vertical steel bars placed at the corners of the fireplace and chimney between the two courses of bricks in 8-inch-thick walls or placed at the corners of the flue between the liner and the brick. At the bottom, the bars are tied to the reinforcement in the footing. Use No. 3 bars in chimneys with a cross-section area of less than 300 square inches; No. 4 bars in larger chimneys.

In addition to the vertical bars, No. 2 horizontal bars should be embedded in the mortar joints at 24-inch intervals, and No. 3 bars should be installed in the chimney cap and at every point where the chimney is anchored to the framework of the house.

Anchorage is required in all chimneys built in or against outside walls. The anchors are made of ¼-inch-thick iron bars embedded in the masonry and nailed to the framing at the roof line and each floor line down to within 6 feet of grade level.

In earthquake regions, the chimney should be reinforced with steel rods and anchored to the framing.

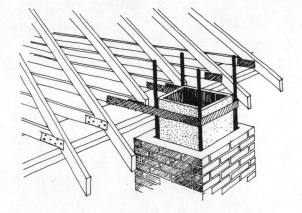

Fireplace Size   Figuring what size a fireplace should be is a knotty problem unless you have an architect to advise you. The problem is aggravated to a certain extent by the fact that you have probably seen (in pictures, if not at firsthand) the large fireplaces our ancestors built in rooms that were often very small. Most of these look attractive; and we must assume that they worked well. "So why," you ask, "shouldn't I build an equally big fireplace in my own home?"

There is no reason why you shouldn't. But before you decide once and for all to do so, you ought to consider a few things:

1. For a fireplace to be as fully effective as a masonry fireplace can be, the fire must heat the back and sides of the firebox so they can radiate heat into the room. This means the flames must more or less fill the firebox; and this, in turn, means that the logs must be almost as long as the back of the firebox.

In the old days, when wood was plentiful, it was no problem for the home owner to cut long logs to fit huge fireplaces. The standard length of cordwood was 4 feet. But today cordwood is usually cut to 2-foot lengths. So unless you have your own woodlot or can buy 4-foot logs, the 2-foot stuff available to you almost forces you to build a small fireplace.

2. The larger a fire, the more air it requires to burn briskly. Here again our forebears had an advantage (if you want to call it that) because their houses were so loosely constructed that ample air seeped in to satisfy a large fire in a large fireplace. By contrast, as pointed out in the preceding chapter, modern houses are too tight to keep a large fire burning. In fact, they're sometimes too tight even to keep a small fire burning. So once again, whether you like it or not, you're almost forced to build a small fireplace.

3. From the appearance standpoint, a fireplace should be in scale with the room in which it's located. If it's too small, it looks silly. If too large, it's forbidding.

But what is proper scale? Here you can get into a debate which is influenced, I suspect, not only by the debaters' personal feelings about what looks right but also by their deep-down, usually unexpressed desires for warmth. My wife, for example, must have much thinner blood than I do because she likes nothing better than to stand in front of a fireplace and toast. I, on the other hand, get about as far away as I can. So I feel sure that, if we were confronted by an oversized fireplace in a small room, she would be

55

Two enormous kitchen fireplaces both built in small farmhouses in the same Connecticut town. (The rooms are no longer used as kitchens.) Both have beehive ovens at the right side (the one opposite now houses house plants; at right it has a cast-iron door, which was added long after the fireplace was built). The paneling and mantel molding opposite are original. At right, both were added about 50 years ago.

Like enormous fireplaces, very small fireplaces have a special charm—and they often turn out to be exceptionally effective heating devices. These are three in point. Fireplace at right is extremely small, in what is now the kitchen of a house built in 1740. It is faced with black-painted concrete. Opposite: a new fireplace set almost into the corner of a bedroom. The two pictures on the next two pages are of the same fireplace, which is also in a bedroom. It's brand new but looks antique because of the wall treatment and because the sides and lintel of the fireplace are made of granite slabs saved from an ancient home.

more inclined than I to say it was in better scale with the room because she would expect it to produce the extra warmth she likes.

Be this as it may, the "rules" for determining the proper scale of fireplaces favor small fireplaces. (I put "rules" in quotes because they're not rules at all; merely opinions.) One that I picked up somewhere in my reading holds that for every square foot of floor area there should be roughly 5 square inches of fireplace opening. The other, which I quote from a Department of Agriculture bulletin, says "a fireplace 30 to 36 inches wide is generally suitable for a room having 300 square feet of floor; the width should be increased for larger rooms."

4. The fireplace should be in general proportion to the wall in which it is set. That is to say, in a wall which is longer than high, the fireplace ought to be wider than it is high. A tall, narrow fireplace would not blend in nearly as well.

5. High fireplaces tend to smoke more than low fireplaces. But I'm not sure that this was always true—otherwise, why would our ancestors have persisted in building so many high fireplaces? (Probably because they found that they produced more heat. And in some cases because they needed height to accommodate cranes and bake ovens.) This leads me to believe that the fault is not with the fireplaces but with the lack of air and possibly the small logs that we must now contend with. In other words, if you can keep a large fire burning briskly, there's no particular reason why high fireplaces should be greater smoke producers than low fireplaces.

6. Fireplaces in second-story rooms are almost always smaller than those on the first floor because they have shorter flues—and as you'll see shortly, the height of the flue has a decided influence on how well a fireplace draws.

All the above statements, of course, are generalizations. They give you only a vague idea of how big a fireplace should be and that, unfortunately, is the best that anyone can do. Planning fireplace size never has been and probably never will be an exact science.

But when it comes to working out the dimensions of a fireplace, we can be a little more definite, although here again you won't find universal agreement. One expert's dimensions are usually different from another's. But as long as you stick to one set of dimensions (that is, if you don't mix Expert A's width dimensions with Expert B's height dimensions and Expert C's depth dimensions), you will come out with a good fireplace.

Before getting into specifics, however, I must digress for a minute to make an important point: Efficient fireplace design does not stop with the width, height and depth of the firebox. You must also consider the dimensions of the forward-slanting back, the size of the throat, the size of the damper, the size of the flue, etc.

Count Rumford's primary interest was not in the aesthetic appearance of a fireplace but in its efficiency as a heating plant. Like most of the better fireplace builders of his time, therefore, he was an advocate of high, shallow fireplaces because they throw out more heat than deep ones. (On the other hand, because the fireplaces are shallow, they do not readily accommodate large-diameter logs, which burn longer. And they are more likely to throw burning embers across the forehearth onto the floor—which means that the forehearth for a shallow fireplace should be somewhat deeper than the 16- or 20-inch forehearth specified for a conventional fireplace.)

U.S.D.A. FIREPLACE DIMENSIONS (Inches)

Opening Width	Opening Height	Depth	Minimum Back (Horizontal)	Vertical Back Wall	Inclined Back Wall	Outside Dimensions of Standard Rectangular Flue Lining
24	24	16–18	14	14	16	8½ x 8½
28	24	16–18	14	14	16	8½ x 8½
24	28	16–18	14	14	20	8½ x 8½
30	28	16–18	16	14	20	8½ x 13
36	28	16–18	22	14	20	8½ x 13
42	28	16–18	28	14	20	8½ x 18
36	32	18–20	20	14	24	8½ x 18
42	32	18–20	26	14	24	13 x 13
48	32	18–20	32	14	24	13 x 13
42	36	18–20	26	14	28	13 x 13
48	36	18–20	32	14	28	13 x 18
54	36	18–20	38	14	28	13 x 18
60	36	18–20	44	14	28	13 x 18
42	40	20–22	24	17	29	13 x 13
48	40	20–22	30	17	29	13 x 18
54	40	20–22	36	17	29	13 x 18
60	40	20–22	42	17	29	18 x 18
66	40	20–22	48	17	29	18 x 18
72	40	22–28	51	17	29	18 x 18

Rumford's rules were rather simple and not overly precise. The width and height of the fireplace opening could be up to three times the depth of the firebox. The width of the back wall should equal the depth of the firebox. The back wall should rise vertically from the hearth for about 15 inches, then slant forward gently to the forward edge of the smoke shelf. The smoke shelf and the throat should be 3 to 4 inches deep. The center of the throat should be directly over the center of the hearth.

The U.S. Department of Agriculture's dimensions are more exact. They are based on modern beliefs that the height of a fireplace opening should be two-thirds to three-quarters of the width; the depth should be one-half to two-thirds of the height.

And here are the dimensions recommended by the Majestic Company, which manufactures such things as dampers and ash dumps as well as prefabricated fireplaces.

MAJESTIC COMPANY FIREPLACE DIMENSIONS (Inches)

Opening Width	Opening Height	Depth	Minimum Back (Horizontal)	Vertical Back Wall	Outside Dimensions of Standard Rectangular Flue Lining
24	28	16	16	14	8½ x 8½
26	28	16	18	14	8½ x 8½
28	28	16	20	14	8½ x 13
30	30	16	22	15	8½ x 13
32	30	16	24	15	8½ x 13
34	30	16	26	15	8½ x 13
36	31	18	27	16	13 x 13
38	31	18	29	16	13 x 13
40	31	18	31	16	13 x 13
42	31	18	33	16	13 x 13
44	32	18	35	17	13 x 13
46	32	18	37	17	13 x 13
48	32	20	38	17	13 x 18
50	34	20	40	18	13 x 18
52	34	20	42	18	13 x 18
54	34	20	44	18	13 x 18
56	36	20	46	19	18 x 18
58	36	22	47	19	18 x 18
60	36	22	49	19	18 x 18

Flue Dimensions

The purpose of the flue in a chimney is to create a draft—a current of air—which carries off the smoke from the fire and simultaneously creates a partial vacuum within the house that causes outside air to enter so that the fire can continue burning. The draft itself is caused by the difference in pressure resulting from the weight difference between the hot flue gases and the cooler outside air. The strength of the draft depends on the chimney height, flue size, and temperature difference between the flue gases and outside air. (Draft is weaker in summer than in winter because the outside air is closer to the temperature of the flue gases.)

Experience and tests have fixed the height of a chimney at the figures previously given (3 feet above the point at which it emerges from the roof and 2 feet above any part of a building within 10 feet). Flue dimensions depend on the area of the fireplace opening and the height of the chimney.

If a chimney, measured from the fireplace throat to the top, is over 15 feet high, the flue opening should have an area equal to one-tenth of the area of the fireplace opening. For shorter chimneys, the flue area should be one-eighth the fireplace opening area.

When you compute the required flue area, if you find that there is no flue tile of exactly that size, use the next size larger tile.

If your home is more than 2000 feet above sea level, increase the flue area and chimney height 5 percent for each 1000-foot increase in elevation.

Special Fireplaces

Special fireplaces include those that are open on two or more sides and those with hoods. All should be designed by an architect or fireplace designer.

MULTIOPENING FIREPLACES   These are particularly difficult to design. In fact, even those designed by so-called experts are not always satisfactory. For one thing, the fireplaces obviously have fewer walls than a conventional fireplace, and these are almost always straight up and down. Consequently, they radiate much less heat into the room.

Because the fireplaces are subjected to cross-currents of air, fires burn more fitfully. There is also a greater hazard from sparks (for which reason, forehearths should be made at least 20 inches deep).

Finally, because the fireplace opening is at least half again as

65

This masonry fireplace is open on this side as well as in front, between the square concrete piers. The throat and smoke chamber are concealed, but the prefabricated chimney is used as an architectural element. (John Fulker)

OPPOSITE *What appear to be four huge stone blocks form this island fireplace. A large prefabricated smoke dome is built into the top block. A low wall of firebrick keeps the logs from rolling backward off the hearth.*
(John Fulker)

large as that of a conventional fireplace, much more air is required to support combustion and draft.

Good solutions to the first two problems have yet to be found. True, if care is taken to locate multiopening fireplaces well away from doors and windows and not directly in the paths of air flowing through them, fickle air currents that interfere with combustion and blow sparks and ashes are less troublesome. Some home owners even go so far as to drop the fireplace and surrounding seating area into a pit below the floor. Nevertheless, the problem remains—as does the radiation problem.

But while lack of air can still be troublesome, burning efficiency has been generally improved by the use of larger flues and prefabricated high-sided smoke domes incorporating a chain-operated damper, oversize smoke chamber and lintel. If fireplace dimensions are taken from these, combustion problems are pretty generally minimized. (For example, if you use a smoke dome with a bottom opening measuring 30 x 16 inches, hearth size cannot exceed 38 x 24 inches. Only the height of the fireplace is variable.)

When a prefabricated smoke dome is used, the fireplace walls are laid up to the opening height decided upon. The flanges on the dome (these form the lintel) are then placed on the walls and set in mortar. The unsupported corner or corners, if any, are set on steel posts. Masonry is then built up around the dome—but with a half-inch space between them to allow for expansion and contraction of the metal—and continued on up around the flue.

A smoke shelf must be provided at the top of the dome, level with the damper. The shelf should be directly below the flue at any side of the dome. The smoke chamber incorporating the shelf has masonry sides which should be covered with a smooth coat of cement mortar to speed movement of the smoke into the flue.

(Smoke shelves are sometimes eliminated in fireplaces built without prefabricated smoke domes. This is particularly true in free-standing fireplaces that are open on all sides. But when this is done, combustion problems are more likely to be the rule than the exception. A common solution is to install a fan in the flue.)

Flue area for a multiopening fireplace is calculated by adding the width of the fireplace openings, multiplying the answer by the height of the openings and then dividing by 12.

Further to insure proper draft, chimney height must be increased. In a house with a pitched roof, the chimney top should

68

ABOVE   A common way of constructing a fireplace with a hood.
TOP   Recipe for a happy evening:
a conversation pit and a large
fireplace with a hood. The fireplace
has no sides; its back is set
forward from the surrounding
wall. (Tile Council of America)
CENTER   This hooded fireplace
is recessed in a large niche with
lights that make reflections on the
shiny ceramic-tile walls. (Tile
Council of America)
BOTTOM   Smoke rises into the
great funnel-like hood and passes
into the chimney flue through the
rectangular connector behind the
hood, at the top. The chain
controls the damper. The slate
forehearth extends far to the sides
and is raised about a foot off the
floor on steel posts. (John Fulker)

TOP   *In hooded fireplaces, the firebox may be flush with the surrounding wall or recessed. This one is slightly recessed. A flexible firescreen follows the lines of the hood.* (John Fulker)

CENTER   *Corner fireplace with a copper hood. The hearth is cantilevered.* (John Fulker)

BOTTOM   *Not all fireplaces that look hooded are in fact hooded. This massive fireplace is of conventional design and has a conventional flue. The chain hanging from the chimney breast controls the damper.* (John Fulker)

extend at least 4 feet above the roof ridge. In a two-story house with a flat roof, the chimney should extend 6 feet above the roof. And in a one-story, flat-roofed house, the chimney should extend 8 feet above the roof.

HOODED FIREPLACES   Fireplaces with hoods are more dramatic than conventional fireplaces, and as the hoods heat up they give off extra heat by radiation and convection. But while use of a hood may simplify construction by the elimination of some masonry work, draft problems may be aggravated—especially in free-standing fireplaces or those which have only a back.

The hoods are generally made of metal—copper, stainless steel, aluminum or painted steel—but are sometimes made of plaster applied over a metal frame, or of masonry. In all cases, they should extend at least 6 inches beyond the limits of the firebox. Metal hoods must be no less than 18 inches from combustible materials.

3 Circulating Fireplaces

If you want a fireplace that "looks as a fireplace ought to look" and really gives off heat, your only choice is a circulating fireplace.

Manufacturers of such fireplaces bandy about figures showing how much more heat their products produce than conventional or prefabricated built-in fireplaces, and if you choose to accept them as gospel, you may. I'm not sure they are derived from adequate testing. But there is absolutely no doubt that the manufacturers' basic premise is correct. All you have to do is talk to someone who owns a circulating fireplace, or visit a house that has one. You'll be amazed how well they heat the room in which they're located. They can even keep an entire house—if small—pretty comfortable.

Whereas a conventional fireplace heats almost entirely by radiation, a circulating unit not only supplies the same amount of radiant heat but also heats the air that is circulated through the fireplace into the room. In effect, the fireplace is a warm-air furnace as well as a radiant heater. And that makes a huge difference in the heat you receive from it.

The effectiveness of the circulating fireplace is particularly noticeable in island or peninsula installations in which the fireplace faces into rooms in front and back. Because such fireplaces—whether of circulating or conventional design—have only two narrow sidewalls, only an infinitesimal amount of heat is bounced off the walls into the room. Even so, the circulating unit raises room temperatures considerably because of the air passing through the shell.

The one possible drawback of circulating fireplaces is that the back wall may be burned out after about fifteen to twenty years. This, however, can be prevented if you build fires in a grate designed to keep the burning wood from making direct contact with the steel; as a result, the life expectancy of the fireplace is comparable to that of a conventional unit. (If repairs are necessary, you can buy a steel plate to cover the fireplace wall.)

What Is a Circulating Fireplace? As noted in Chapter 1, a circulating fireplace is a prefabricated firebox made of steel. It has an inner wall which forms the lining of the firebox, containing the heat and reflecting it into the room.

73

It also has an outer wall separated from the inner wall by an air space a couple of inches wide. Air enters this space through grilles installed at floor level. As it is heated by the inner wall, it rises through the space and flows back into the room through grilles above the firebox.

In addition to the firebox, the circulating fireplace shell incorporates the throat, a high smoke dome and damper. Consequently, it serves as a complete fireplace form that assures good draft (assuming, of course, that the flue and chimney are properly proportioned) and greatly simplifies the mason's work. Despite the latter advantage, however, the cost of a complete installation is not a great deal different from that of a conventional fireplace and chimney. The $200 you pay for a firebox with a 3-foot-wide opening is but a fraction of the total cost.

74

Types and Sizes Circulating fireplaces are available with a single front opening; an opening in front and at either side; and an opening in front and back.

Sizes are fairly limited but include those for which there is greatest demand. Front-opening units range from 30 to 71 inches wide, 16¾ to 23 inches deep and 25 to 37½ inches high.

Corner units are 31 to 38 inches across the front, 20 to 24 inches deep and 27 inches high.

Front-and-back-opening units are 34 or 42 inches wide, 24 inches deep and 21 inches high. Unlike the other designs, these have steel hearths which are built into the shell at the factory.

Construction Circulating fireplaces require the same kind of foundation as conventional fireplaces. The hearth is also the same except in front-and-back-opening units. An ash dump is optional. The shell is placed on the hearth and surrounded with 1-inch-thick mineral wool insulation to prevent expansion of the steel from cracking the surrounding masonry, which is made of common bricks or stones. If your building code permits, the bricks (or stones) need be only 4 inches thick; but for some large fireplaces, an 8-inch thickness is required in the back wall.

The flue and chimney are generally built in the usual way but in some cases a prefabricated metal chimney is used. The flue must not rest directly on the fireplace shell. For fireplaces opening in front and back, the chimney should be capped (see page 144).

Air Inlets The placement of the openings that admit and discharge air from the fireplaces depends on the design of the fireplace, whether it is flush with the wall or projecting, and where you want the heat to go.

In front-opening and corner fireplaces, the inlets are installed in the sides of the fireplace (in a corner fireplace, one of the inlets is in the open end of the back). Consequently, if a fireplace projects from the wall, the inlet openings in the wall are generally centered on those in the shell. In a fireplace that is flush with the wall, on the other hand, the openings are placed in the wall on either side of the shell. In fireplaces with raised hearths, the inlets are installed below the hearth on either side of the fireplace opening. The hearth should be elevated at least 15 inches. In all cases, the inlets are placed at floor level.

76

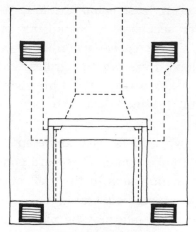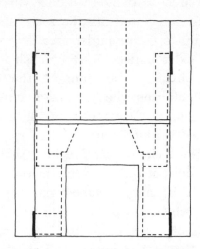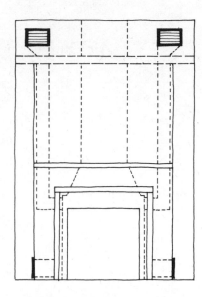

Here are several ways in which the inlets and outlets for a circulating fireplace can be installed. At left, the fireplace is flush with the wall. Inlets are placed under the raised hearth; outlets in the wall. In center drawing, the fireplace projects from the wall and both the inlets and outlets are placed in the sides of the projection. At right, the fireplace projects from the wall. The inlets are in the sides of the fireplace; the outlets carry heat to the floor above.

The wall openings are connected to those in the shell by smooth-finished, cement-parged ducts built through the masonry or by metal ducts. The area of the ducts must be the same as the area of the openings in the wall and shell. Metal grilles are available from the fireplace makers to cover the wall openings. But you may construct your own grilles of bricks or stones. The bricks or stones should not be more than 1¼ inches wide and should be spaced 1½ inches apart. The combined area of the openings between the bricks or stones must be no less than the area of the duct or inlet in the shell. That is, if the inlet shell measures 8 x 12 inches (96 square inches), a wall opening with a grille of 1¼-inch bricks must measure 8 inches high by 20¾ inches long to provide the same area.

To increase the volume of air moving through the largest circulating fireplaces and thus to build the proper pressure to help the fireplaces function most effectively, electric fans (available from the fireplace maker) can be installed behind the wall grilles. (The need for fans in small fireplaces is questionable, however.) The fans must be placed in both inlets for a balanced air flow.

A front-and-back-opening fireplace is always raised off the floor 15 inches or more. The air inlets are placed under the forehearth in front and back of the fireplace. Air flows from the inlets though ducts into a large open space under the steel hearth. Here it picks up some initial heat. As it flows up through the steel walls at the sides of the fireplace, it is heated further.

Air Outlets The area of the outlet ducts and the grills through which the heated air flows into the room should at least equal the area of the inlets. If the outlet area is greater because you install one or two extra outlets, inlet area should be increased accordingly or you should install fans in the inlets. Here again, grilles are available from the fireplace manufacturer to cover the wall openings; or you can construct grilles of 1¼-inch bricks or stones spaced 1½ inches apart.

Most circulating fireplaces have two outlets located in opposite sides of the shell just below the smoke dome. These are connected by smooth-walled masonry or metal ducts to the wall outlets, which are placed either in the fireplace wall or in the side walls of a projecting fireplace. The wall outlets may be placed at any height, but since warm air rises, it doesn't make sense to put the outlets just below the ceiling level. You will feel warmer if they are several feet lower. But they must be high enough so that the ducts connecting the outlets from the shell to the outlets through the wall rise at a 30-degree angle at least.

Another possible location for the outlets is in the top of the mantel shelf. In this case, the vanes in the outlet grilles, which are located at the ends of the shelf, are adjusted to direct the warm air across the wall away from the fireplace.

The Heatform fireplace made by Superior differs from others in that it has two outlets in the sides as well as a single large outlet in the front. The latter directs air into the room through a grille located 9 to 12 inches above the fireplace opening. You can use either the side outlets or the front outlet, or you can use all three if you increase the number of air inlets.

One of the primary advantages of circulating fireplaces is that they can be used to heat adjoining rooms on the same floor and/or floor above as well as or instead of the room in which they are located. This is accomplished by running ducts from the outlet grilles in the sides of the shell though the wall behind the fireplace, through walls close to the sides of the fireplace or up through the chimney and into the room or rooms directly overhead. Several outlet arrangements are possible: (1) One outlet in the room with the fireplace and the second in another room; (2) two outlets in the fireplace room and one or two outlets in another room; (3) both outlets in an adjoining room; (4) one outlet in one adjoining room and another outlet in a second adjoining room; (5) one or two outlets in the fireplace room, one outlet in an adjoining room and another outlet in a second adjoining room.

However, if the fireplace is used to circulate air through more than two outlets, steps must be taken to insure that there is ample air moving through the fireplace. The easiest way to do this is to install fans in the inlets (one manufacturer recommends installing fans in the outlets). Another way is to order a fireplace shell with a third inlet opening in the back of the shell to bring in air from the room which you are heating at the rear of the fireplace.

(Note that even though you install more than two outlet grilles, there are never more than two outlet ducts connected to the fireplace. This means that one duct is connected to two grilles.)

Converting a Conventional Fireplace to a Circulating Fireplace

This is possible to do in some fireplaces but not all, because the dimensions of the old and new units must be more or less similar. The simplest installation is made with a Superior Heatform, since the outlets are located in the front of the shell and there is no need to construct outlet ducts through the sides of the existing fireplace. Even so, the work is extensive and calls for an expert. The facing and firebrick lining must be removed. The lintel, if too low, must be raised. Air inlet ducts must be constructed. The smoke shelf may have to be reconstructed. Then, after the shell is set in place, the warm air outlet must be installed and the fireplace breast and facing rebuilt. The cost of all this can run up into the high hundreds of dollars.

4 Prefabricated Built-in Fireplaces

Prefabricated built-in fireplaces are a relatively new development but they have taken hold with a vengeance for several reasons:

1. Installed, they look just like a conventional fireplace. Without making a close-up examination, you would, in fact, be hard put to tell the difference.

2. They're inexpensive. Prices for fireplaces start at about $300, and the chimney adds almost the same amount. This, of course, is for materials alone. Installation by a carpenter might add $100 or more, depending on the complexity of the work. Even so, the cost is well under that of conventional and circulating fireplaces.

3. They are easy to install yourself. Under ideal circumstances, you might even get the whole job done in a weekend.

4. They can be installed just about as easily in an old house as a new one. What's more, you can locate them almost anywhere without extensive reconstruction of the house or great cost. And they take up little space—even less, in fact, than many smaller free-standing fireplaces.

What They Are A prefabricated built-in fireplace is a completely assembled steel firebox with a built-in smoke dome, damper, hearth and flexible draw-type firescreen. The shell has double or triple walls separated by a space or spaces through which outdoor air circulates to keep the outer wall cool. An air space is also provided under the hearth. Further to insulate the firebox and protect the steel from the flames, the bottom, sides and back are lined with fire-resistant refractory material.

The chimney is of comparable design. Prefabricated out of steel in easy-to-handle sections, it is nothing more than an oversize flue with double or triple walls separating air spaces that insulate the surrounding framework from the high-temperature gases given off by the fire.

Because of this elaborate construction, prefabricated fireplaces now on the market can be placed hard against combustible surfaces without any danger of igniting them. In the manufacturer's par-

A built-in prefrabicated fireplace framed and faced with beautifully joined random stone blocks. The forehearth, which serves as a bench on either side of the fire-place—and even turns the corner in the right foreground—is made of the same stone. (John Fulker)

A type of metal fireplace used in the past when there was no space for a full-size fireplace. It's a cast-iron shell without a back that was placed against firebrick. A hole in the brick just below the flat top of the shell vented smoke into the chimney. In this instance, the firebox is only 9½ inches deep and is recessed in the wall only 5 inches. The owner evidently had trouble at one time with flying embers, because he extended the forehearth with brick, then extended it further with a sheet of copper.

lance, they require "zero clearance." The chimneys require a clearance of only 2 inches.

While most built-in fireplaces heat entirely by radiation, there are several of circulating design. Some of them take in air through an inlet below the hearth, circulate it through the shell and return it to the room through an outlet below the lintel. One design can be equipped with a fan to increase the volume of air. Another manufacturer offers a model with a fan connected to the flue. This forces outdoor air down through the walls of the flue, through the walls of the firebox and out into the room. Ducts can be connected to the sides of the fireplace to carry the heated air into adjoining rooms.

One of the peculiarities of built-in fireplaces is that, because of the insulating air space below the hearth, the hearth must be raised several inches above the floor. Consequently, the normal inclination is to raise the forehearth to the same height. If you do this, however, you create a ledge that is easy to stumble over. So

Prefab fireplaces are generally raised off the floor. The one above has a false front (available as an optional trim kit) which makes it look much wider than it really is. (Martin)

The kitchen fireplace below has no forehearth but is set behind an 8-inch masonry wall. (Heatilator)

it's better either to recess the forehearth in the floor or to raise the fireplace and forehearth a foot or more so the change in elevation is more apparent. (If you install a circulating built-in fireplace with an air inlet below the hearth, the forehearth must be lower than the hearth.)

Another peculiarity of built-in fireplaces is that the back is straight up and down rather than slanted forward. As a result, it radiates slightly less heat into the room than a conventional or circulating fireplace. In addition, there is no way to install a smoke shelf; so there is more chance for downdrafts to blow soot into the room and disrupt the fire.

Sizes and Designs

The selection of built-in fireplaces is limited to front-opening and corner designs in just a few sizes.

In front-openers, the opening is 28, 36, 42 or 48 inches wide (overall width is 38, 46, 52 or 58 inches) and 21 to 27 inches high. The firebox is 18 inches deep.

Corner fireplaces, which are open at either the left or right end, are 36 or 42 inches across the front and 18 inches deep.

Locating a Fireplace

You can build a prefab fireplace against an interior or exterior wall so it protrudes all the way or only partway into the room; in a corner, island or peninsula. You can also build it into an outside wall flush with the inner surface. In this case, the fireplace and chimney are enclosed in a chase, which is, in effect, a box extending from the bottom of the fireplace—or from the ground—to just below the top of the chimney.

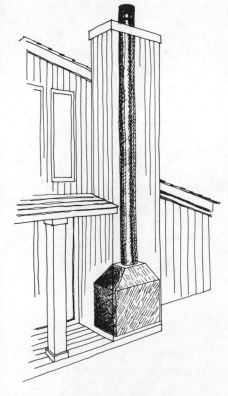

A built-in fireplace installed, with the chimney, in a chase built against the outside wall of the house.

Although considerable material (usually wood, though it might be brick or stone) is required to construct a chase, this kind of installation is in many ways the easiest to make since you don't have to run the chimney up through the ceiling and roof. Instead, you just cut and frame an opening for the fireplace in the exterior wall. The chimney runs straight up through the chase.

When making an inside installation, you should run the chimney up between the joists and rafters so these don't have to be cut. This means the fireplace should, ideally, be centered below the openings cut through the ceiling and roof, because then you don't have to go to the trouble of making offsets in the chimney—it can be as straight as an arrow. But if this makes it impossible to center the fireplace on a wall or locate it exactly where you want it, don't

Some prefabricated built-ins are open at the front and either side. (Preway)

worry. A prefabricated chimney can be constructed at an angle of as much as—but no more than—30 degrees from the vertical without affecting the draw. (The total length of one or more angled runs, however, must not exceed 15 to 20 feet, depending on the manufacturer.) Thus, it's possible to locate the fireplace almost anywhere. For instance, you can place it directly under a fireplace on the second floor and angle the chimney up around a second-story bathroom or to one side of the roof ridge. Similarly, if a straight chimney would come up through the middle of a room on the second floor, you can bend it so that it's against a wall or in a corner, where it can be concealed. You can even bend it up through a closet.

Installing a Fireplace Because prefabricated fireplaces and chimneys are relatively lightweight (only about 600 to 700 pounds total), you don't have to build a massive foundation for them. If a floor is solid—as most adjacent to exterior walls are—you can set the fireplace on it with-

85

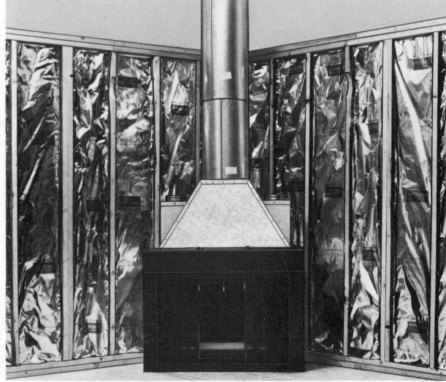

Four steps in the corner installation of a prefabricated circulating fireplace. First it's set in place and blocked so it cannot move. Then the prefabricated metal flue is installed.

The wall across the corner is framed. Finally the air inlets (with fans) are connected at the base and the outlets are installed at the top of the wall. (Heatilator)

out additional preparation. If the fireplace is to be placed on a sagging or weak floor within the house, however, you should shore up the floor with lally columns or wood posts. If it is to be installed in a chase without foundation walls, the floor should be cantilevered, as shown in the drawing.

The platform for a raised fireplace is a simple framework of two-by-fours anchored to the floor and covered with half-inch plywood.

Construct the forehearth of ⅜-inch-thick noncombustible materials such as brick, marble, slate, ceramic tile or hollow metal. This, too, can be laid right on a floor. If it's recessed, cut out the finish floor with a circular saw, being careful not to cut into the subfloor.

In all cases, the bricks, etc., in the forehearth should be cemented down with adhesive like that used for setting bathroom tiles. Apply it with a notched trowel and press the bricks into it firmly. The joints between bricks are ⅜ to ½-inch wide. Trowel a wet mixture of 1 part masonry cement and 3 parts sand into them and pack it down flush with or slightly below the surface. Make sure the joint between the hearth and forehearth is completely filled.

The chimney is built before the fireplace is enclosed. (More on this below.)

Set the fireplace in its proper position. It does not have to be fastened, but you should nail two-by-fours to the floor on both sides and in back so it cannot shift. (In some California communities, however, a fireplace must be securely anchored to the hearth as earthquake protection.)

Frame the walls around the fireplace with two-by-fours spaced 16 inches center to center. If the fireplace facing is to be flush with the wall, the studs for the wall must be set back from it a distance equal to the thickness of the wall-surfacing material. Example: If you intend to cover the wall with half-inch gypsum board, the studs must be a half inch back from the surface of the fireplace facing.

In most installations, the wall surrounding the fireplace opening has no load-bearing function; consequently, the opening in the wall can be framed as in drawing below. But when a fireplace is built into an exterior wall (or an interior bearing wall), the header

How to cantilever a floor to support a chase.

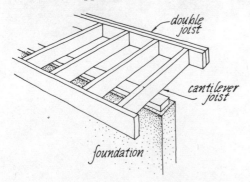

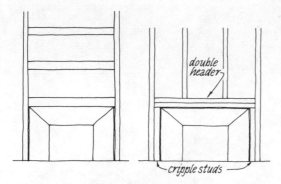

double header

cripple studs

If the wall around and above the face of a built-in fireplace does not support the structure above, it can be framed as at left. But if the face of the fireplace is flush with a bearing wall, the wall must be framed as at right.

framing the top of the wall opening must be doubled and supported on cripple studs as in drawing above.

Before surfacing the walls around the fireplace, the fireplace should be grounded so that, if lightning should strike the chimney, the electrical charge can be bled off safely. To do this, secure a No. 6 copper wire to the back or side of the fireplace shell with a bolt. Clamp the other end of the wire to the metal pipe that supplies water to the house. If a plastic pipe is used to bring in water, fasten the wire to a ground rod driven 6 feet into the ground outside the house.

Cover the framing around the fireplace and chimney with any type of wall-surfacing material—gypsum board, plywood, hardboard, brick, etc. If the material is noncombustible, it can be extended over the front edges of the fireplace shell to the edges of the opening in the shell. Combustible materials, however, must not overlap the facing. Instead they should be installed flush with the facing and butted against the outer edges of the fireplace shell (see the manufacturer's directions, however).

If combustible wall-surfacing material protrudes beyond the fireplace opening (that is, if it extends further into the room than the facing), it must be set back from the sides of the fireplace opening at least 6 inches and must be set above the top of the opening at least 12 inches (again, see the manufacturer's directions). A mantel shelf must be at least 12 inches above the top of the opening.

The facing used for prefabricated fireplaces is usually made of black-painted steel and comes with the fireplace. But you may apply a facing of ceramic tile, marble—anything noncombustible. Stick it to the fireplace shell with dry-set Portland cement.

An easy way to give the traditional masonry look to a prefab fireplace is to cover the wall with imitation stone or brick. The stone must, however, be fireproof if it is placed as close to the fireplace opening as this. (Z-Brick)

Installing the Chimney

The chimney for a built-in fireplace must be extended above the roof according to the rules given in Chapter 1.

Buy the chimney designed for the fireplace from the fireplace dealer. The number of sections required and their length depend on how high the chimney rises above the roof and whether it is straight or angled. The accessories required to make the installation also depend on whether the chimney is straight or angled and on the number of floors it must pass through.

The pieces used in the construction of a chimney include:

1. Straight pipe sections in 12-, 18-, 24- 36- and 48-inch lengths. Some manufacturers also offer a section that is adjustable in length.

2. A starter section used to connect the straight pipe to the fireplace. Not all fireplaces require one. The sections are straight or angled at 15 or 30 degrees.

3. Elbows used to change the direction of the chimney. They are angled at either 15 or 30 degrees.

4. Chimney tops to finish off and protect the chimney and to keep rain and drafts from blowing down the chimney. They are either round or square.

5. Chimney housings made of enameled metal to resemble a brick chimney. Used solely to improve the appearance of the chimney, they will house one, two or three flues.

6. Flashing collars placed around the chimney to keep water from dripping through the roof. Since they are designed for roofs with different slopes, you must determine the pitch of your roof before placing your order. To do this, hold a carpenter's spirit level horizontally against the side of the roof; measure out along it 12 inches from the roof; then measure straight down to the roof. If the vertical measurement is 4 inches, the roof has a 4-inch pitch.

7. Firestop spacers used to center the chimney in holes made through floors and also to prevent flames from roaring up through the chimney enclosure in the event that the house catches on fire. These are made for chimneys rising straight or at a 15- or 30-degree angle from perpendicular.

To order the components for a chimney that is straight from bottom to top, measure the distance from the rooftop to the floor of the room in which the fireplace is located; subtract the total

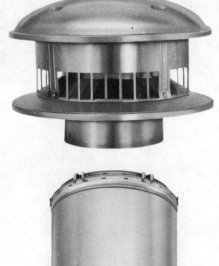

A section of a prefabricated chimney and a chimney cap. All parts of prefab chimneys are light in weight and designed to slip together easily and quickly. (Wallace-Murray Corp.)

height of the fireplace, and add the projection of the chimney above the roof. This sounds simple enough to do, but in order to arrive at an accurate answer, it will probably be necessary to make holes in the ceiling under the roof and through any floors through which the chimney passes.

Figuring for a chimney that has offsets is more difficult.

After establishing the position of the fireplace, mark its center on the floor. Drop a plumb line from the ceiling to the center mark and make a corresponding mark on the ceiling. Find the exact position of the ceiling joists between which the chimney will rise. Make marks on the ceilings showing the inside edges of both joists. Measure from the center mark on the ceiling to the joist marks.

Measure the height of the ceiling. Also measure the distance from the ceiling to the top of the roof and add the distance the chimney will project above the roof.

Take all these measurements to the fireplace dealer and ask him to figure out which chimney components you need. But don't be surprised if he tells you that, for one reason or another, the installation cannot be made as planned—that the location of the fireplace must be shifted an inch or two or even a foot or two. If that should happen, let him have a look at the house to find a new location for the fireplace or chimney or to advise you what must be done to make the installation originally planned.

Once you and the dealer have determined which chimney parts you need, the actual installation is relatively simple.

First cut holes through the ceiling, floor above and roof. The sides of the holes should be flush with the sides of the joists and rafters. The length of the holes should equal their width. After the holes are cut, frame them by nailing 2-inch-thick timbers the same width as the joists or rafters between the joists or rafters at the ends of the holes.

Remember that there must be a space of at least 2 inches between a prefabricated metal chimney and all adjacent combustible materials. If you do not have this much clearance, one of the joists or rafters must be cut out. To support the cut pieces remaining, nail headers to their ends and to the joists or rafters on either side of the enlarged opening. The headers should be of the same thickness and width as the joists or rafters. (See drawing.)

Begin construction of the chimney by installing the starter

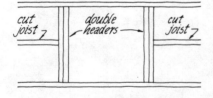

How to frame an opening in a floor for a prefabricated chimney if it's necessary to cut a joist.

RIGHT *Instead of using a prefabricated chimney housing, the owners of this house enclosed the chimney in redwood boards matching the house walls.*
OPPOSITE *Here a prefabricated chimney is also concealed with boards. The window in the side of the chimney lets light into the rooms below.* (Moore, Grover, Harper, architects)

section over the outlet in the fireplace shell and fastening it into place according to the manufacturer's directions. Above this, install standard straight sections one after the other until the chimney extends to the proper point above the roof. All pieces used are interlocking, with the bottom of the upper piece fitting down around the top of the piece below.

Where the chimney passes through a ceiling, a firestop spacer must be centered and nailed over the framed opening (usually over the bottom of the opening). The chimney is then inserted through the hole in the spacer.

At the roof, the flashing collar is placed over the framed opening, and the flanges are slipped into place under the shingles at the top and sides of the hole. The bottom flange rests on top of the shingles. The collar is then secured with nails driven through the collar and fastened to the section below.

If a decorative chimney housing is used, cut off its bottom at an angle to match the pitch of the roof. Then fasten the housing into place according to the maker's directions.

Finally, install the chimney cap.

Round chimneys that extend more than 5 feet above a roof should be braced with a piece of ¾-inch metal conduit nailed to the roof on the high side of the chimney. The conduit is bolted to a metal band that is clamped around the chimney.

When a section of chimney is installed at an angle, secure a 15- or 30-degree angle (as needed) to the chimney section or fireplace just below the bend. The elbow should, of course, be angled in the direction the chimney is to go.

At the top of the bend, install another elbow pointing in the opposite direction. The elbow used at this point should be equipped

Several ways in which a prefabricated chimney can be extended up to and through the roof.

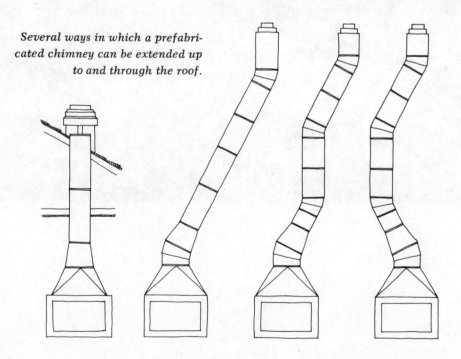

with hanger straps which are nailed to the joists or rafters above so the chimney cannot sag. Angled chimney sections exceeding 6 feet in length should also be supported at 6-foot intervals with metal straps or heavy wires that are looped tightly around the sections and nailed to the framing.

The distance that a chimney can be offset depends on the combination of elbows and straight chimney sections that you use. The smallest offset is made with a pair of 15-degree elbows set one directly above the other. The lower elbow points one way; the upper one, the other.

For a slightly greater offset, use a pair of 30-degree elbows in the same way.

For still greater offsets, start with a 15- or 30-degree elbow pointing to the right; add a straight section of the desired length; and finish with a second elbow like the first but pointing to the left.

5 Free-standing Fireplaces

I have an abiding affection for the Franklin stove, descended from Ben Franklin's wonderful creation. When I was younger, I spent many months in the northern Maine woods; and the stoves were as much a part of life as wood-burning cookstoves, canoes and fishing rods. They spelled both comfort and companionship. Even with a small fire burning in the grate, they gave off a tremendous amount of heat to all sides. In the early evening, when the stove doors were open, they cast flickering, leaping shadows on the walls. When I went to bed and closed the doors, they kept the cabin cozy pretty much throughout the night.

And despite their black, old-fashioned solidity, they somehow imparted to the cabin—with its moss-chinked walls, worn floors and uncomfortable straight furniture—a strange sort of charm.

I don't think that any of the modern free-standing fireplaces inspired by the Franklin stove can measure up to it in beauty. None holds a candle to its efficiency. And that's undoubtedly why Franklin stoves are still made and still popular.

But this in no way detracts from the merits of the many Franklin progeny that are now on the market. They have a very definite role to play in today's homes—as the scores of thousands of home owners who have bought them will attest.

For one thing, they cost considerably less than all other types of fireplace. And since they're not built in and the chimneys need not be built in—their installation cost is relatively low. In fact, the smallest, simplest fireplace (which costs about $150) can be purchased and installed for $350 to $400.

They are much easier to install than even a prefabricated built-in fireplace. One day's work should do the trick if the chimney is of simple design.

For both of these reasons, they permit you to have fireplaces in several rooms. In addition, you can locate them anywhere within the rooms.

And their sleek, modern, colorful design is ideally adapted to contemporary homes.

This modern-day Franklin stove is the central feature of an enormous two-story kitchen. Rather than venting it directly into the brick chimney, the owners used the flue as a dramatic feature and ran it up to within about 5 feet of the cathedral ceiling.

What They Are The free-standing fireplace is a complete lightweight (roughly 90 to 400 pounds) unit that is ready to start heating your home as soon as you set it on a fire-resistant base and put in the chimney.

The fireplace is essentially a box—usually oddly shaped—with few of the draft- and smoke-controlling features of a conventional fireplace. In the great majority of units, smoke from the fire rises straight up the chimney. The damper, if any is in the chimney. One fireplace, however, incorporates a built-in damper and smoke shelf.

The box is made of sheet steel or, in a few cases, cast iron. Only the hearth is lined with firebrick or other refractory material. The walls and top are a single, unprotected thickness of metal; consequently, they become too hot to touch and must be placed well away from combustible walls. But if you want the maximum amount of heat, they're the top choice because they radiate heat in all directions. This is particularly true of cast-iron fireplaces. (Another advantage of cast iron is that it lasts much, much longer than steel.)

Other free-standing steel fireplaces either have double walls with insulation packed in between or are lined on the sides as well as the bottom with refractory material. Because of this, they don't suffer from the drawbacks of the single-wall units, but don't give off as much heat.

In all free-standing fireplaces except Franklin stoves a firescreen is built in. Almost all are finished in a tough red, yellow, green, etc., enamel.

Designs Half of the fun of owning a free-standing fireplace of modern design is in listening to the exclamations and comments of your friends. All the fireplaces are conversation pieces. Some are undeniably cute—they look diminutive even though they may actually be larger than many conventional fireplaces. Their color is eye-catching—not at all characteristic of what we usually think of as a fireplace. And they're shaped and installed in entrancing ways.

The shapes range from neat rectangular cubes to—well, words do not describe some of the others. There are pyramids, spheres, teepees, balls, cylinders, hourglasses. And of course there's the good old Franklin which has rather the look of Ben himself, standing straddle-legged, with hands folded over protruding belly, as he

100

TOP *Rectangular fireplace with something of the look of the Franklin stove but definitely of modern design.* (Martin)
BOTTOM *A large teepee-model free-standing stove. The extra metal surface gives off just that much more heat.* (Malm)

Two fireplaces designed for corner installation. (Right, Malm; below, Western)

RIGHT *Most free-standing fireplaces are finished in a tough, glistening, colorful enamel.* (Temco)

BELOW *Some free-standing fireplaces are even suspended from the ceiling.* (Malm)

discourses patiently with the British about their iniquities. It's a fascinating display of the modern designer's skills when he lets himself go.

The direction in which a fireplace radiates heat into the room varies with the shape of the shell. Many units are open only in front. Many others have an opening which sweeps across the front and part way around the sides—like a fish mouth. A few are open all the way around.

To add to this multiplicity of styles, some fireplaces stand on the floor; some are mounted on the wall; and one or two hang from the ceiling on chains.

In short, you may find it difficult to pick out the model that appeals to you most.

Sizes

Sizes are completely unstandardized. If you must have a fireplace that fits into a certain space, the only thing you can do is look at all the models that are for sale.

The smallest unit I've been able to find is a Scandinavian design on legs that measures 20 inches wide, 35 inches high and 19 inches deep. The largest is a 44-inch-diameter teepee that is 90 inches high.

A rough average size is 34 inches wide, 42 inches high and 29 inches deep. Note, however, that these are outside dimensions. Width and depth measurements include forehearths; height measurements include whatever pedestals the fireplaces stand on. For example, the intermediate size Franklin stove measures 38 x 32 x 25 inches overall; but the firebox measures only 25½ x 18¼ x 15. This means, obviously, that most free-standing fireplaces take up considerably more floor space than they seem to at first glance.

Locating a Fireplace

As indicated earlier, the amount of space required for a free-standing fireplace also depends on the construction of the firebox—whether the walls are insulated and/or lined with refractory material or whether they are made of a single thickness of steel or cast iron.

Some units can be placed hard against all types of wall; that is, they are installed with zero clearance. Some can be placed against noncombustible walls only. Others must be placed a specified distance from both combustible and noncombustible walls. For example, one make of Franklin stove must be installed a minimum of 36 inches from a combustible wall behind it; 24 inches

OPPOSITE *This large free-standing fireplace is designed so it can be placed directly against a combustible wall.* (Western)

104

Even though a free-standing fireplace is raised off the floor, you must cover the floor with fireproof material extending well in front and to the sides of the opening. Here, the stove stands on a bed of marble chips. (Martin)

from a combustible side wall. However, if an optional heat shield is installed, the distance to the back wall can be reduced to 18 inches (side-wall distance remains 24 inches). On the other hand, if the surrounding walls are noncombustible, the clearances for the stove can be reduced to 6 inches.

What is a combustible wall, and what is a noncombustible wall?

A combustible wall is one that catches fire easily or conducts heat. Under this definition, which is approved by the National Fire Protection Association, combustible materials include wood, plywood, hardboard, particleboard, fiberboard, gypsum board, metal, plastics, cork, acoustical board and tile, *as well as* all walls covered with paint, glaze coatings, clear finishes such as varnish, wallpaper, vinyl wallcovering and all other flexible wall coverings.

A noncombustible wall is one that does not catch fire easily or conduct heat. Materials include *bare* (unfinished) brick, stone, concrete and concrete block, plaster, asbestos-cement board, ceramic tile and glass.

The only other limitation on locating a free-standing fireplace is the design of the chimney and flue connecting it to the fireplace. This is discussed a little further on.

Installing a Fireplace   This is child's play. The only thing you have to do before setting the fireplace in position and constructing the chimney is to cover the floor, if combustible, with noncombustible material. Although some manufacturers do not clearly call for this, it is necessary under all fireplaces regardless of how high they are placed above the floor, because: (1) it protects the floor from the heat emanating from the bottom of the firebox (this, however, is less of a problem with some fireplaces than with others); and (2) it catches flying embers, for even though many free-standing fireplaces have built-in forehearths, these are not deep enough to contain all sparks.

The dimensions of this noncombustible base must conform with the dimensions given in Chapter 1 for conventional fireplace forehearths: the base must extend a minimum of 16 inches in front of the fireplace opening and a minimum of 8 inches beyond both ends of the opening.

You can build the base on top of the floor or recess it. Use brick, stone, marble or ceramic tile and fill the joints with fire-resistant mortar. The thickness of the material should be at least ⅜ inch; however, if you use marble chips, as some people do, they should be at least 2 inches thick.

All free-standing fireplaces should, of course, be level. If the floor slopes, build up the base to compensate.

The fasteners used to hang fireplaces on a wall or from a ceiling must be driven into the framework of the house. If they are simply driven into a wall or ceiling between studs or joists, they may not be capable of supporting the fireplace, particularly in an earthquake.

Installing a Chimney

Unlike other types of fireplace, free-standing units are not connected directly to the chimney. Instead, the chimney starts at the ceiling or roof above the fireplace or at an outside wall; and the space down to the fireplace is filled with an uninsulated, single-wall flue pipe, or "stove pipe." This is called the chimney connector.

You can buy connector pipes and elbows in the same color as the fireplace from your fireplace dealer. Just make sure they are made of 24-gauge, corrosion-resistant metal; the thin stuff so often used is likely to be riddled with holes by the flue gases. The dealer also has the necessary components for the chimney. Unpainted connector pipes and chimney components that can be used with any type and make of fireplace are also available from building-supplies outlets. If you buy from one of these sources, you must make certain that (1) the chimney is an "all fuel" design which is not only capable of continuous operation at a 1000-degree flue-gas temperature but can also withstand 1400-degree temperature for one hour (the same kind of chimney can also be used with pre-fabricated built-in fireplaces and circulating fireplaces); (2) the connector is made of 24-gauge steel; and (3) the inside diameter of the connector and chimney is no larger or smaller than that specified for the fireplace.

Components used for free-standing fireplace chimneys include those described in the previous chapter as well as the following:

1. Collars, or faceplates, to cover the openings around flue pipes where they pass through ceilings or walls.

2. Support boxes which support and center the chimney in the wall, ceiling or roof from which it takes off.

3. Tees used to connect a horizontal connector pipe to a

chimney. The base of a tee has a removable cap to permit cleaning the chimney and draining off water that may enter through the top.

4. Brackets which support chimneys running up an outside wall.

Venting of free-standing fireplaces is done in several ways:

1. The connector pipe is run straight up to the ceiling where it is joined to the chimney that continues straight up through the roof.

2. The connector is run straight up to the ceiling where it joins the chimney. From there the chimney is angled up to the roof and then rises straight through the roof.

3. The connector is carried up to a point a little below the ceiling, where it makes a 90- or 45-degree bend and continues across the ceiling until it makes another bend into the chimney, which goes straight up through the roof. (In no case should a connector have more than two bends.)

4. The connector is run straight up from the fireplace to the ceiling, makes a 90-degree turn, and continues to an outside wall. Here it is connected to a tee from which the chimney extends up the outside wall past or through the roof overhang.

5. The connector runs straight back from the outlet of the fireplace to an outside wall, where it connects to a tee from which the chimney runs up the outside wall. (In some Franklin stoves, the outlet can be placed in the back of the fireplace for even more direct connection to a chimney.)

6. The connector is run into an unused flue in an existing chimney.

In all cases where a connector pipe is installed horizontally, the pipe must be sloped upward at least ¼ inch per foot and the length of the run should not exceed 75 percent of the height of the chimney above the connector. This second rule is at variance with the early practice of running the pipe across the ceiling for great distances in order to take advantage of the heat given off through the walls of the pipe. The main reason for the change is to assure that the pipe does not lose so much heat that the draft is affected.

Another rule that you must observe when installing the connector is that it must not be run through a wall, ceiling or roof

The flue for a free-standing fireplace can be run straight up through the roof or across the room to an outside wall, as here.

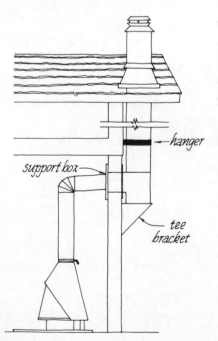

support box

hanger

tee
bracket

and must be spaced at least 18 inches out from any combustible surface that it parallels.

If you vent a fireplace into an unused flue in an existing masonry chimney, a metal or tile thimble is first inserted in the hole made through the chimney wall and flue liner. This is fastened in place with fireclay. The connecter pipe is then slipped into the thimble far enough to hold securely without cementing. Neither the liner nor the connector should extend beyond the inner face of the flue liner.

Since the chimney for a free-standing fireplace is separated from the fireplace, it can be installed either before or after the fireplace. Just start at the support box or wall bracket at the bottom end and build up (see Chapter 4).

Installation of the connector involves nothing more than cutting the pipe sections to the required length; slipping them together and securing the joints with sheet-metal screws or rivets, and then fitting the ends over the outlet of the fireplace and into the chimney. If the connector has a horizontal run made up of two or more sections of pipe, support it from the ceiling with wires or straps.

6 Gas and Electric Fireplaces

If you're thinking of putting in a fireplace to cut heating costs, you're not likely to give much thought to one that burns gas or electricity. That's like jumping from the frying pan into the fire. Nevertheless, such fireplaces are selling briskly as auxiliary sources of heat—and hang the cost of operation. They fill this purpose well. Especially the electric fireplaces. As a heating fuel, electricity is far and away the most efficient known. Furthermore, every BTU of heat a fireplace produces enters the room. Since there is no need for a chimney, no heat is lost up the flue.

Gas fireplaces are considerably less efficient. For one thing, one unit of gas produces only about 0.8 unit of heat. And much of the heat escapes to the outdoors via the flue, which is essential.

On the other hand, gas logs produce flames—not such large, active, colorful flames as wood, but flames nonetheless. If you enjoy a fireplace for the beauty of the fire, a gas fireplace is infinitely more attractive than an electric, which produces only a glow combined sometimes with a man-made flicker.

Finally, since gas is generally somewhat less expensive than electricity, a gas fireplace is cheaper to operate (but you can never tell when this may change).

Gas-burning Fireplaces

Any existing fireplace—conventional, circulating, built-in or free-standing—can be made into a gas fireplace simply by having a gas pipe run into it and connecting this to last-forever gas logs. But if you're installing a fireplace for the first time, it saves money to buy a free-standing or prefabricated built-in gas-burning fireplace.

All free-standing fireplaces can be used to burn gas instead of wood. As in an existing fireplace, you just make a hole in the back, side or bottom (some fireplaces come with knockout holes) and install a gas line and gas logs. A few free-standing fireplaces, however, are designed specifically for gas. The most unusual is a wall-mounted unit with a small built-in "furnace" in addition to the gas logs. The furnace supplements the heat from the logs when the temperature plummets.

Prefabricated built-in fireplaces made specifically for gas differ

112

This gas fireplace, designed to hang on a wall, has an auxiliary heater in the base. (Temco)

from their wood-burning counterparts in one important respect: since they have a much shallower firebox, they take up less space. In overall length, they range from 38 to 60 inches. Overall height is 30 to 33 inches. Only front-opening units are made. Cost runs about $100 less than that of a wood-burner of corresponding size.

Forehearths are not needed with most gas-burning fireplaces; but this should be verified by the dealer before you make an installation.

The chimneys used with gas-burning free-standing and built-in fireplaces are constructed out of prefabricated metal components like those for wood-burning units—with two differences:

1. The inside diameter of the flue pipe is only 4 or 5 inches—half the size of the flue for a wood-burning fireplace.

2. Since the chimney does not have to withstand such intense heat, it has only a double wall with a single air space between. Called a Type B chimney, it is suitable for venting only gas fireplaces and appliances. (The connector pipes used with gas-burning fireplaces are ordinary stove pipes with a single wall.)

Connector pipes for gas-burning fireplaces are installed according to the directions given in the preceding chapter. For installation of the chimney, see Chapter 4; however, only 1-inch clearance is required from all combustible materials. Accordingly, a 5-inch round chimney with an outside diameter of 5½ inches can be installed in an enclosure measuring only 7½ x 7½ inches.

If you use an oval vent pipe, even less space is required. (The pipe is not really oval, but has flat sides and rounded ends.) It is possible, in fact, to run the chimney up through a standard 2 x 4-inch-stud wall.

In all cases, the chimney is terminated with a large cap designed to prevent downdrafts. Because of this, it need not project above the roof as high as the chimney for a wood-burning fireplace. On chimneys up to 12 inches in diameter, the horizontal distance from the sides of the cap (which extend several inches beyond the sides of the chimney pipe) to the roof must be a minimum of 2 feet. The vertical distance from the lowest discharge opening in the cap to the roof must be a minimum of 1 foot for roofs with a pitch up to 7 inches; 1½ feet for roofs with an 8-inch pitch; 2 feet for roofs with a 9-inch pitch; 2½ feet for roofs with a 10-inch pitch; 3¼ feet for roofs with an 11-inch pitch; and 4 feet for roofs with a 12-inch pitch. Roofs with greater pitch require still higher chimneys; and if there is a vertical wall within 8 feet of the chimney, the chimney must extend at least 2 feet above the top of the wall.

Electric Fireplaces

Just by placing a ready-built assembly of 20-inch electric firelogs in a grate or on fire dogs and plugging them into an outlet, you can make any fireplace into an electric heater. The cost is only about $40.

But the big call for electric fireplaces is in houses and apartments that don't have a fireplace and by people who don't want to go to the trouble or expense of building a fireplace and chimney. So quite a few complete electric fireplaces are made.

All are free-standing in the sense that you don't have to build them in, but a few look like built-ins. These resemble conventional fireplaces that project from the wall; but the bricks or stones are molded out of fiberglass. The mantel shelf is made of wood or fiberglass. The fireplaces measure 52 to 60 inches long, 37 to 42

Some electric fireplaces look like the real thing, but the bricks are made of fiberglass and the entire unit weighs very little. No flue is required. (Fasco)

Wall-mounted electric fireplace gives off a flickering orange-red glow and, of course, gives off heat as well. (Martin)

inches high and 20 to 22 inches deep (including the built-in fiberglass hearth). There are also units that fit diagonally across a corner of a room and measure 52 inches wide by 37 high.

All other electric fireplaces are true free-standers. Cones which are set on the floor any distance out from the wall are 30 or 31 inches wide and deep and about the same height. All come with a metal chimney, which is painted the same color as the fireplace. This is strictly for ornament.

Other free-standers are hung on the wall. They run from 25 to 34 inches wide; 38 to 55 inches high; and 12 to 15 inches deep. A few have fake chimneys.

The wattage and heat output of electric fireplaces varies considerably, so if you're looking for maximum comfort, shop the field. The heat is given off by the logs themselves; and in some cases, there's an additional heater in the base below the hearth. Most units operate at 120 volts; some at 240. You can plug them into an outlet with an extension cord; but it obviously looks better to run a cable in through the wall.

The fireplaces do not require forehearths or noncombustible bases on the floor.

7 Stoves

The essential difference between a fireplace and a stove is that the latter has doors across the opening so that the fire is completely enclosed. Because of the doors, the draft in a stove is subject to much finer control and, as a result, the stove makes much more efficient use of fuel and produces much more heat over a longer period of time. The heat is transferred to the air circulating through the room by the superheated walls and top of the stove as well as by the stove pipe. At the same time, the stove and pipe heat by radiation.

One load of wood in a really well-designed stove can keep an entire house of five or six rooms warm for up to 12 hours. Of course, most stoves are not this efficient. Even so, when a stove is strategically placed in a room, it emanates heat in every direction. Much of this passes through the doorways, walls, floor and ceiling into the adjacent rooms. And after a while, conditions throughout a large part of the house range from perfectly comfortable or even overheated in the room with the stove to pleasant or tolerable in the other rooms.

Naturally, if you don't want house-wide comfort from a stove, you can use a smaller or less efficient stove just to heat a single room. But even in this situation, you will get better performance with less work and at lower cost from a stove than a fireplace. Initial cost is also lower, starting at $90 for a simple model.

The only thing you won't get—except from the Franklin stove and a couple of new models with tempered glass doors—is the pleasure of watching the fire burn.

What They Are

In its simplest form, a stove is an enclosed cast-iron or steel box with a fire burning in the bottom. Air for combustion is admitted through adjustable openings in the front or top. The smoke and gases are carried off through a vent and up the chimney.

But there's considerable difference between the simplest stove and the advanced designs that are now available. For one thing, the simple stoves admit a certain amount of air around the doors, whereas the advanced designs are almost totally airtight, giving you much more accurate control of the fire and greater efficiency.

118

Adding to the efficiency of many of the advanced designs is a system of baffles that control air movement through the stove. Because of this, the gases given off by the burning wood burn along with the wood, thus increasing the amount of heat produced and reducing the damage done by the gases to the flue.

In advanced designs damper control is built in instead of being installed in the stove pipe.

In a few stoves, there are even thermostats that automatically open and close the damper just enough to maintain the level of warmth you have selected. And at least one stove can be equipped with an electric blower which pulls the heated air down through the cabinet and forces it out at floor level, thus giving more even heat throughout the room.

Whatever its design, a stove requires less attention when in operation than a fireplace. Once you light the fire and set the vents and damper, it will usually burn for several hours before you need to add more fuel. In the morning, the ashes are shoveled out or shaken down into an ash drawer; more fuel is added; and the stove is ready for another day. People who depend entirely on stoves for warmth never let the fire go out from fall till spring.

Wood is most commonly used for fuel. The more seasoned it is the better, because it not only burns more efficiently but also produces less creosote, which may gum up the chimney and catch fire. The length of the logs used depends, of course, on the size of the stove. (One disadvantage of many stoves is that you may not be able to buy logs in the required length and must therefore recut them yourself.)

Bituminous coal and coke can also be used for fuel, but only in a few stoves. Some of these are designed for coal or coke exclusively. In a few others, you can use either coal, coke or wood—even peat.

Sizes and Shapes

If you think free-standing fireplaces are variable in size and shape, you'll be amazed at the even greater variety you will find in stoves. Much of this variety is attributable to foreign designers. American manufacturers stick pretty much to simple cubes and pot-bellied designs, but the Scandinavians let their imaginations roam—usually with handsome results. For all I know, the Chinese, French and Patagonians are equally fanciful; but so far they haven't bothered to cater to the U.S. market as the Scandinavians have. The latter

119

Three American-made stoves that allow you to watch the flames as they put out heat to all sides. (Top, Monarch Kitchen Appliances; center, Self-Sufficiency Products; bottom, Fire-View Distributors)

Stoves made in the Scandinavian countries come in many unusual shapes and are usually highly ornamented. They're also usually very efficient. (Scandinavian Stoves)

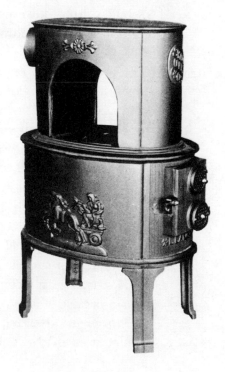

even make a big thing of decorating their stoves with bas reliefs of moose, horses, spruce trees—you name it.

The largest stove I've come across is the good old Franklin. The biggest Ashley—the best-known American-made high-efficiency stove—is not too far behind. It measures approximately 35 inches wide, 21 deep and 36 high. The smallest is a Norwegian model that burns wood, coke, coal or peat. It's only 13 inches wide, 12 deep and 32½ high. There's an American potbelly that would be even smaller than this if you could remove it from its spread-eagled base.

Building Your Own Stove

For your home, you're not likely to try building a stove yourself, because the design and fabrication of an attractive unit are not that readily mastered. But for the workshop or a rustic ski lodge, you might be tempted.

All you need for an extremely simple wood-burning stove is a 55-gallon steel drum, a flue and a kit (sold by one of the larger stove makers) including two pairs of legs, a heavy-duty door with draft assembly and a stove-pipe flange.

A more elaborate stove designed to burn sawdust is described in U.S. Forest Service Research Publication No. NE-208 (write to the Forest Service, U.S. Dept. of Agriculture, 6816 Market Street, Upper Darby, Pennsylvania 19082). This is made of a 55-gallon drum, an inner 30-gallon drum and about $25 worth of other materials, including the flue.

Locating a Stove

There was a good reason why old storekeepers put their stoves smack in the center of their stores: to spread the heat into every corner. Most home owners today don't go as far as this even when the stove is their only source of heat. But it's obvious that, if you want maximum comfort, the best place to put a stove is in a free-standing position well out from a wall or corner.

Such a position is, in fact, mandatory if the walls of the room are combustible. Unlike free-standing fireplaces, stoves are never built for zero clearance from combustible walls. A clearance of about 3 feet is required (see your local building code and the stove manufacturer's specifications for the exact spacing).

If a wall is noncombustible, on the other hand, you can set a stove as close to it as you wish.

Stoves are also frequently placed in front of existing masonry fireplaces so they can be vented directly up the chimney. When

OPPOSITE *Ideal location for a stove is in center of room so it can radiate heat in all directions.* (Kristia Associates)

122

In an effort to beat the rising cost of fuel, the young owners of this home closed up their fireplace and installed a wood stove. The fireplace opening was closed with copper and the wall was faced with brick to protect it from heat. The extended forehearth is slate. The copper-covered, leather-cushioned bench is a woodbox.
(A.J. Hand)

this is done, the fireplace opening is sealed shut with brick, asbestos-cement board or a steel sheet; and the vent pipe from the stove is inserted through a hole in the center.

When locating a stove, if you're planning to use it to heat more than one room, thought must be given to the size and location of the room.

A room near the center of the house is obviously preferred to one in a corner or wing.

A large room with several doorways is better than a small room or a room with only one doorway, because the heat is more easily transferred to the rest of the house and the room itself will not get so warm.

However, even if the room in which the stove is located does not meet these requirements, it is possible to heat a sizable part of the house without overheating the stove room by either or both of the following measures:

1. To heat the upstairs, install a large grille in the ceiling above the stove.

2. To heat adjacent rooms, install grilled openings or low-speed kitchen fans high in the walls of the stove room.

If a stove is installed in the basement to heat a small house, the basement walls should be insulated from the ceiling down to the normal frost line; and grilles should be placed in the floors of the rooms above.

Installing a Stove   Stoves are installed almost exactly like free-standing fireplaces.

Despite the fact that most stoves are raised well off the floor on legs, the floor underneath should be covered with ⅜-inch-thick non-combustible material. A forehearth extending at least 18 inches in front of the stove opening and 8 inches to both sides is required. If ashes are removed from the side of a stove, a forehearth must extend 18 inches in front of the ash-removal door.

No reinforcement of the floor is necessary since the weight of even the largest rarely exceeds 350 pounds.

The chimney should be either masonry or an insulated prefab unit which extends above the roof to the heights specified in Chapter 2. The stove should be placed as close as possible to the chimney and connected to it by a connector pipe of the heaviest metal available. The rules given for connector pipes in Chapter 5 apply also to those for stoves.

8 Remodeling Fireplaces

After Count Rumford developed his theories about fireplace design, he spent some time in England rebuilding fireplaces. This was relatively easy to do since the British fireplaces were large, deep, rectangular boxes with throats large enough for a chimney sweep to squeeze through; so all Rumford and his employees had to do was build new brick walls with a narrow throat within the fireplaces.

The average American fireplace cannot be remodeled so easily because it is much smaller and is already designed more or less to Rumford principles. Nevertheless, there is nothing you cannot do. I justify that sweeping statement on the ground that, if you can't actually remodel a fireplace, you can tear it down and start over again from the top of the foundation.

Fireplace remodeling, however, is not for amateurs (except as they may change the size of the opening by the methods discussed in the next chapter).

Remodeling of a chimney—whether to change the dimensions of the flue, add to the bulk of the chimney to make it more attractive, install a clay liner in an unlined chimney or attach a new chimney to an old one—is also a professional job.

Types of Remodeling

Although I have written about home remodeling and repair for almost forty years, I always have some trouble making a distinction between the two, because much remodeling involves repairwork. In the final analysis, however, remodeling means to make a definite change in a structure, whether this be to correct a defect or to improve the performance or appearance of the structure and any related structures.

Using this definition, here are some of the ways you can remodel a fireplace or chimney.

1. Change the appearance of the mantel and wall immediately surrounding the fireplace.

2. Change the forehearth or fireplace facing.

3. Change the design of the firebox, throat and smoke chamber.

4. Increase the exterior dimensions of the chimney to make it look better. Inside chimneys are enlarged from the top down to a

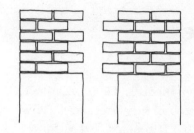

If you join a new chimney to the side of an old chimney, the bricks above the roof should be interlocked so the two chimneys appear as one.

point just below the roof; outside chimneys are generally enlarged from top to ground.

5. Add to the height of the chimney by building up from the present top or by installing chimney pots.

6. Build a new fireplace with a new chimney added to the end or side of an existing chimney. When this is done, the bricks in the new chimney should be "toothed" into the old chimney by removing the half bricks at the end of every other course in the latter. Only in this way can the two structures be made to look like one. If you simply erect the new chimney next to the old and tie them together with cement, there is an arrow-straight dividing line between the two.

7. Install a prefabricated fireplace within the firebox of an existing fireplace to increase efficiency.

8. Convert a fake fireplace which served as the background for a stove into a real fireplace. But this usually calls for a complete tearing down of the old fireplace and chimney because the flue required for a stove is smaller than that required for a fireplace.

Changing a Mantel

This is a simple job and one that more home owners should undertake, because an appalling number of mantels are hideous. Traditional mantels in various stock designs and sizes are made of wood or urethane. You can also buy old mantels from junkyards and antique dealers (a few of these specialize in fireplaces and stoves). Or you can engage an architect to design a mantel or, if you're reasonably clever, design one yourself.

Old mantels made of masonry materials are the most troublesome to remove, because they are generally cemented directly to the fireplace. (Heavy stone mantel shelves, in fact, are built into the fireplace and may be well nigh immovable.) But with hard work, you can chip them off bit by bit.

Wood mantels, on the other hand, are nailed to framing built around the fireplace, and it usually takes only a few minutes to pry them off.

Installation of the new mantel then proceeds fairly rapidly. It is essentially a cut-and-fit process. If the wall is framed, you just nail the mantel to this. If the wall is masonry, drill holes for lead anchors, and secure the mantel to the anchors with screws.

The one thing to make sure of is that the proper clearances between the mantel and fireplace opening are maintained.

128

RIGHT *If you're looking for authentic mantels of an earlier era, you can often find them in antique shops—particularly those specializing in fireplace fittings. This mantel came from such a shop and has since been used in two homes.*
BELOW AND PAGES 130 AND 131 *Four antique mantels which were recently sold by a dealer. The handsome pedimented paneling above the mantel shelf on page 131 is called an over-mantel.* (Edwin Jackson, Inc.)

Mantel Shelves Usually when a mantel is replaced the shelf is replaced, too. But sometimes a mantel shelf alone is replaced, which means that you just pry off the old and nail on the new.

The easiest way to make a mantel shelf deeper so you can place, say, a large clock on it is to cut a board of the appropriate thickness to the desired dimensions and nail it right on top of the old mantel. The joints between the two mantels can then be trimmed, as you like, with stock wood moldings.

To put a mantel shelf on a fireplace that doesn't have one, you can buy one of the numerous prefinished shelves which are on the market or cut it out of lumber. The shelf is supported by and attached to the wall with wood or metal brackets, which are available in great variety in lumberyards.

Hoods Unless a fireplace is specifically designed for a hood, you can't add a hood that will serve a functional purpose without having a mason rebuild the fireplace. But there's no reason why you can't install a purely decorative hood.

Remember, however, that if the hood is to look functional (it would look absurd otherwise), it must extend down over the top of the fireplace opening. For this reason, it cannot be constructed of wood, plywood or any other combustible material. It should, instead, be made of copper or other sheet metal; plaster on metal lath; or asbestos-cement board that is fastened at the joints—to a point at least 12 inches above the fireplace opening—with steel angles.

Whatever the construction of the hood, it can be fastened to the wall above the fireplace with screws driven through concealed flanges into the studs.

Refacing a Fireplace If you dislike the old facing that surrounds the opening of a masonry fireplace, you can replace or conceal it with a new facing of thin marble or slate, ¼-inch-thick bricks (but not of the plastic or fiberglass variety), opaque glass, ceramic tile or any other noncombustible material you can think of.

If the old facing is of brick or stone, the new material is applied directly over it. Other facings, such as marble, can also be covered but are usually removed.

The first step is to scrub the old facing thoroughly with tri-

132

The marble surround for this fireplace is an old one taken from a house built in New Jersey at the time of the Revolutionary War. It was probably carved in France. At one time it was painted with innumerable coats of black paint.

sodium phosphate to remove dirt, soot, grease, etc. Rinse well and let dry. Scrape off all paint except that sunken in the interstices of the facing.

The best material for attaching the new facing is a dry-set Portland cement which comes ready-mixed with sand. Mastics like those frequently used for tiling walls are strong and tenacious, but might be weakened by the heat. If the old facing is reasonably smooth and level, apply the cement, after mixing with water, with a notched trowel with notches $\frac{3}{32}$ inch deep. But on a rough and uneven facing, first apply a skim coat over the entire surface to make it smooth and level. For this, use a trowel with a smooth edge. When this is dry, apply a second coat with a notched trowel.

133

Set the new facing material at once and push it in firmly so that the ribbons of cement are spread out over the entire back of the facing. If necessary, brace the facing until the cement dries. If applying ceramic tiles, those at the top of the fireplace opening should be supported along the bottom edge on a board so they cannot slip.

After the cement has dried, grout the joints between the pieces of facing material with a cement grout like that used in a ceramic tile wall.

Facing a prefabricated built-in fireplace can be done only by tack-welding expanded steel lath to the fireplace, covering with Portland cement mortar, and applying the facing to this with dry-set mortar.

Resurfacing Forehearths

Even though it means that the forehearth will project above the surrounding floor, it is much easier to lay a new surface directly on the old than to remove the old surface, which is firmly embedded in concrete.

For the new hearth, you can use ceramic tile, marble, slate or ¼-inch bricks. Set the material with dry-set Portland cement as described above or with a ceramic tile mastic.

Often one of the easiest ways to change the appearance of the fireplace surround is to cover it with ceramic tiles. (Tile Council of America)

Both the surround and forehearth were faced with ceramic tiles, and the tiles were continued up the wall and around a window cut in the wall to expose the outside chimney. (Tile Council of America)

9 Improving Fireplace Draw

If the fire in your fireplace fills the room with smoke and burns sluggishly, it is for one of three reasons:

1. If you've had trouble from the first time you ever used the fireplace, it's probably because the fireplace was improperly designed or constructed.

2. If the trouble began after you had been using the fireplace for some time, it's probably because the chimney and smoke shelf need cleaning or have developed faults or because of something you have done in the house.

3. And there is always the possibility that the wood you're using is of poor quality.

Whatever the reason, the odds are that you can correct the problem. But you may not succeed without some experimentation. And it's possible that you will have to call in a qualified fireplace builder to make major alterations in the firebox, throat or smoke chamber.

Improve the Air Supply
Insufficient air is today the cause of a huge number of smoky fireplaces. When you weatherstrip doors and windows to prevent heat loss from your house, you cut down the air supply in the house. When you put on storm windows, add insulation in the roof, walls and floor, install vapor barriers, you reduce the air supply further. Meanwhile your furnace is gobbling up enormous quantities of air; and every time you turn on the ventilating fan in the kitchen, more air in the house is lost.

Because lack of air is such a common problem in modern homes, it's the first thing you should worry about when your fireplace smokes. The corrective measures to take are pretty obvious:

1. Build your fire on andirons or in a grate. Simply by raising the fire off the hearth, you increase the amount of air circulating around it; quite often this is all you have to do to improve combustion and stop smoking.

2. If your ventilating fan is running while the fireplace is in use, turn it off or close the door between the kitchen and the room with the fireplace.

3. Open a window in the room in which the fire is burning. You don't have to open it very wide to make a big difference in the air supply. If the wind is blowing, the open window should be on the windward side of the room. This may sound illogical and unpleasant, but there is a sound explanation: As the wind passes over the house, it creates a vacuum on the leeward side; and if a window on this side is open, the vacuum will probably draw air out of the house instead of increasing the supply within.

If you find that opening a window perks up the fire and puts an end to its smoking, you ought to think about installing a duct to bring air directly to the fireplace from the outdoors so you can keep the windows shut. For how to do this, see Chapter 1.

Clean the Smoke Shelf

The purpose of a smoke shelf is to deflect the air that flows down the chimney back up. But it does this only if it is clean. When soot builds up on it, the incoming air spills off into the fireplace, causing the flames to sputter and smoke to puff out into the room.

To clean the shelf, try to disengage the handle from the damper. It's held sometimes only by a cotter pin. Lift out the damper. You can then brush the soot from the shelf. If the damper is hard to remove, reach up behind it with your vacuum cleaner hose.

Scrape the soot from the damper and free up the pivots on which it turns at the same time.

Clean the Chimney

A heavy accumulation of soot and creosote in the flue can cause smoking by restricting the upward movement of gases. It may also catch on fire. Consequently, you should make a practice of cleaning the chimney regularly—once a year if you use your fireplace fairly frequently; every six months if you have a daily fire. It's a simple enough job if you don't mind clambering around over roofs.

The usual cleaning method recommended to do-it-yourselfers is to put a couple of bricks in a burlap bag, stuff the bag with straw or leaves, and tie it to the end of a stout rope. Drop the bag into the chimney and haul it up and down until the soot is rubbed off.

This method is reliable only in straight flues. For that reason, chimney sweeps prefer a second method, which works both in straight and angled flues. It is much more effective in removing creosote, which becomes caked on to the walls of the flue, than a burlap bag.

Tie a chain—an old tire chain is excellent—to a rope and scrape this up and down the walls of the flue. When going around bends, waggle it back and forth—not too violently—so that you clean all sides of the flue.

To keep the soot that rains down from the chimney from flying out of the fireplace, be sure to cover the fireplace opening with an old sheet or piece of plywood.

After cleaning the flue, you must clean the smoke shelf and damper. Then pick up all the soot that collects on the hearth and dump it into a garbage can.

Several ways of cleaning chimneys with chemicals are used, but none works as well as the manual methods. Furthermore, they involve some risk of chimney fires since the soot is actually burned out. For this reason, the chemicals should be used—if they are used at all—three or four times a year, before a flue has become heavily encrusted, rather than once every year or two, after the deposit has become thick.

Rock salt is one of the most popular chemicals, though it is not terribly effective. Use two or three cupfuls.

Metallic zinc in the form of dust or granules is another cleaner, but not much better than salt and harder to come by. A mixture of salt and zinc is better than either alone.

Old flashlight batteries can be used, too. They work best if chopped into pieces.

All these materials are scattered on a moderate fire and allowed to cook for about fifteen minutes. Then build up the fire briefly.

Check the Chimney for Cracks

This should be done about once a year, because cracks can cause triple trouble. By letting cold air leak into or around a flue, they upset the draft. By letting out hot gases and perhaps sparks, they may start a fire in the structure surrounding the chimney. And by letting water into the masonry, they cause the gradual disintegration of large sections of the chimney.

The best way to inspect for cracks is to build a smoky fire in the fireplace; block the top of the flue with a wet blanket; and look for smoke seeping out of the sides of the chimney. But unless you have reason to suspect the chimney is in bad shape, there is generally no need to do this more than once every two or three years. In the in-between years, just make a close-up visual inspection of the chimney walls.

138

All cracks and weak mortar joints you find should be plugged promptly. Scrape them open as much as possible and blow out the crumbs. Dampen with water. Then pack into them a damp mixture of 1 part masonry cement and 2½ parts sand.

Fixing cracks that extend through the chimney wall into the flue is not such easy business; but fortunately you may not have to do anything about them for years if you keep the cracks well sealed on the outside. However, if and when you can no longer do this, positive action is indicated.

If the cracks are so far down the chimney that you can't get at them from the top, your safest course is to have the chimney rebuilt. But sometimes a mason can seal a crack by dropping a bag stuffed with straw into the chimney below the crack; pouring a viscous cement grout onto the bag, around the edges; then working the grout into the crack by pulling the bag up and down.

Reduce the Fireplace Opening

If none of the measures described so far has any appreciable effect on your fireplace, more drastic measures are called for. The first step is to determine whether the fireplace opening is too large in relation to the flue, because if it is, the volume of air entering the fireplace cannot be carried off and some of it pushes back into the room.

There is a simple but effective way to make this determination. Build a fire in the fireplace. Hold a wide board or piece of plywood across the top of the fireplace opening, and gradually lower it until the smoke stops billowing into the room. Make a mark on the fireplace facing at the lower edge of the board. You now can do several things.

1. If you normally use the fireplace without a firescreen, place a screen across the opening. It should fit fairly tightly so that all large air passages are blocked. (A flat, draw or hood-type screen is preferable to a folding screen.) This may reduce the amount of air entering the fireplace sufficiently to prevent further smoking.

2. If the screen doesn't work, you should reduce the actual opening size by raising the hearth, installing a hood across the top of the opening or building a tier of bricks up both sides of the opening.

Raising the hearth is the easiest procedure and has least effect on the appearance of the fireplace. It is also a good way to make a further test of the effect that a smaller opening has on the

OPPOSITE *To improve the draw of this 200-year-old fireplace, the owner built up the hearth by one layer of brick.*

smoking problem. As a starter, you can use any bricks that happen to be handy. Lay these close together on the hearth, covering more or less the entire surface (don't worry about small gaps between the ends of the bricks and the angled sides of the firebox). The thickness of the layer should equal the distance from the top of the opening to the mark you made at the bottom of your test board. Spread a layer of sand under the bricks if necessary to achieve this thickness.

Now build another fire to make sure the smoking problem is licked. If it isn't, raise the bricks a little more. If it is, remove the bricks and put in a permanent hearth of firebricks laid in fireclay.

Installing a hood across the top of the fireplace opening is equally effective but it alters the appearance of the fireplace— sometimes unfavorably. What most people do is to have a copper or painted steel hood made by a sheet-metal worker. This is then fastened into the opening with screws driven into lead anchors set into the sides of the firebox. You can, however, achieve the same result with a long steel angle (a length of heavy structural steel bent lengthwise into a right angle) screwed to the underside of the opening. Or if you want to go to the trouble, you can install a new steel lintel and lay bricks on it.

Reducing the width of the fireplace opening is usually done only if the size of the opening must be cut down so much that a raised hearth or hood would make an objectionable change in the appearance of the fireplace. Use firebricks and cement them to the sides of the firebox, flush with the front edges, with fireclay. You need only a single tier on both sides of the opening; don't completely cover the sides from front to back.

Increase Chimney Height

If your fireplace smokes only on windy days, the chimney is pretty certain to be the cause of trouble.

The first and easiest thing you can do about it is to make sure that the flue projects a few inches above the top of the chimney and that there is a beveled layer of cement extending from just below the top of the flue to the surrounding edges of the chimney top.

The second solution is to add to the height of the chimney; but since this is a major job, it should be undertaken only if careful measurements show the chimney to be lower than the rules in

RIGHT *Chimneys can be capped with large semi-circular tiles or metal sheets.*
BELOW *Chimney capped with a slab of stone. A withe separates the two flues.*

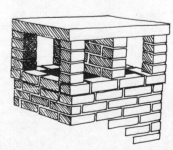

Chapter 2 call for. Even if this is the case, it is still smart to make a test of what will happen when you make the addition.

To do this, buy a piece of flue tile the same size as the chimney flue and a little longer than your measurements indicate. Stand this on top of the chimney and anchor it securely with sandbags and wires attached to the surrounding roof. Don't try to anchor a second length of tile atop the first if the latter doesn't stop the smoking.

If the test works, you should call in a mason to build the chimney higher or to install decorative chimney pots.

Cap the Chimney If your chimney smokes on windy days despite the fact that the chimney has a properly beveled top and meets the chimney-height rules, it very probably can be corrected by the addition of a hood that deflects winds away from the flue.

Hoods can be designed in several ways, but most home owners settle for the simplest—one they can build themselves, if they're strong enough. This is nothing more than a flat slab of slate or flagstone supported above the chimney top on four little brick piers. But you must make sure that the openings under the slab have a combined area at least equal to the area of the flue.

If the chimney has two or more flues, each flue must be separated from the other by a small wall of brick called a withe. And the openings surrounding each flue must have a combined area at least equal to the area of the flue.

To construct the hood, lay up a brick pier at each corner of the chimney with masonry cement. Wet the bricks with water before embedding them in the cement. Then secure the slab to the tops of the piers with masonry cement.

Install a Draft Inducer A draft inducer is an electric fan enclosed in a weather- and heat-proof metal housing which is anchored to the top of a chimney flue. It is turned on and off by a switch installed somewhere in the house—probably next to the fireplace. In operation, it works like a kitchen exhaust fan, pulling the smoke from the fire up the chimney and exhausting it to the air even in the face of strong wind currents. Because it creates such a powerful draft, a better-than-average volume of fresh air must be brought into the house to keep the fire burning.

It's not likely that you will need a draft inducer to correct a

144

smoking problem in a conventional front-opening fireplace, because the simpler and, for the most part, less expensive measures described above usually do the trick. But smoking in multiopening fireplaces is much more difficult to control, and a draft inducer is often the only answer.

10 Correcting Other Fireplace Problems

Poor combustion and smoking are not, alas, the only problems you may have with a fireplace. There are many others—some serious, some simple; some easy of solution, some not.

Heat Loss Up the Chimney

One of the purposes of a damper is to keep heat from the house from escaping up the flue when the fireplace is not in use. But since it's made of iron, which transmits heat and cold readily, it does this job only moderately well. So if you don't use your fireplace often, it pays to stuff a piece of mineral-wool or fiberglass insulation into the throat of the fireplace below the damper. Just remember to remove it before you start a fire.

Thermostat Out of Kilter?

If the thermostat for your heating system is installed in the room with a fireplace, don't blame it if the rest of your house feels cold when you're burning a fire. It's the fireplace that's causing the trouble.

What happens is this: The fire raises the temperature of the room. At the same time, the air from adjoining rooms flows toward the fireplace, thus lowering the temperature in those rooms while helping to raise it in the fireplace room. As a result, the thermostat turns the heating plant off long before the rest of the house is heated to the desired temperature; and it turns on the heating plant after the temperature in the rest of the house has dropped well below the desired level.

The solution to the problem is obvious: Move the thermostat into another room where it won't be affected by the fireplace.

Loose Bricks in Firebox

Bricks in a firebox sometimes come loose and fall out. In ancient fireplaces, they may be literally eaten away by the heat. To replace one, break it free of the surrounding masonry and chip out the mortar left on the adjacent bricks. Chip out as much mortar as possible from the bottom of the hole. Then sprinkle all sides of the hole with water and spread fireclay into the bottom and up the sides slightly. Set in a new firebrick, after wetting it well with water, and tap it firmly into the mortar until it is flush with the

146

surrounding surface. Then trowel fireclay into the joints, pack it in solidly, and trowel it off flush with the surface.

Loose Bricks in Chimney

A loose or broken brick on the face of a chimney is removed and replaced as above. Use 1 part masonry cement and 2½ parts sand for mortar.

In unlined chimneys, bricks may loosen and eventually tumble down the flue. Luckily, it is usually the bricks in the upper part of the chimney, where the heat is greatest, that do this, so you may be able to reach down the chimney and set in a new firebrick with fireclay. But if the brick is out of reach, there's nothing you can do except have the chimney torn down and rebuilt from that point up. This is clearly a major undertaking and major expense. However, if the flue is larger than it need be, it may be possible to line the chimney with an insulated metal flue or tile liner.

Persistent Wet Spots on Chimney Walls

Check the chimney cap for cracks. If there are any, chip off the concrete and replace it. Bevel it away from the top of the flue toward the edges of the chimney.

The wet spots may also be caused by water getting into open joints in the sides of the chimney. Chip these open and fill with 1 part masonry cement and 2½ parts sand.

Leaks Through Roof Around Chimney

The chimney flashing is in need of attention. If it has holes, clean the metal with steel wool and smear on an epoxy metal mender. If the metal is torn, bring the edges together; steel-wool the metal until it glistens; brush on an acid flux; and apply solder. If the flashing has pulled out of the mortar joints in the chimney, clean the joints well; fill them with 1 part masonry cement and 2½ parts sand; and press the metal firmly into the mortar.

Walls Around Chimney Unusually Hot

Extinguish the fire at once and don't build another until you have a mason make an inspection. There are undoubtedly cracks in the chimney, and until they are repaired, you're in danger of setting the house afire.

Smoke Leaks from One Flue into Another

This can happen if the flues are not separated by a tier of bricks and if the joints in the flues are cracked. You obviously can't improve the separation. But you can seal the joints by grouting them with a straw-filled bag (see page 139).

147

Efflorescence on Chimney

Efflorescence is a crusty white powder that forms on brick and other masonry. It is no more common on chimneys than on walls, but because of the prominence of chimneys and because they are often the only masonry structure on houses, it is more noticeable.

The efflorescence is caused by moisture within the masonry, so the first thing you should do is to check the chimney for cracks through which water may be entering and seal them.

To remove the efflorescence, scrub with water and a stiff brush. If this doesn't work, use a solution of 1 part muriatic acid in 9 parts water, and scrub this on with a fiber brush. Then rinse immediately and thoroughly. The efflorescence may or may not return.

Soot on Fireplace Face

Scrub with a strong solution of trisodium phosphate. If stains remain, use a weak solution of muriatic acid.

Damper Broken

Disconnect the handle, lift out the damper plate and replace it.

Birds and Squirrels Invading Chimney

Cover the top of the flue with a half-inch or coarser square wire mesh. If this is folded well down around the sides of the flue, it need not be anchored further.

Loose Joints in Stove Pipe

If the pipe sections have simply slipped apart or sagged, bring them together properly; drill a couple of holes through the joint; and drive in short sheet-metal screws.

If smoke issues from a loose joint, put a couple of turns of duct tape, made for heating systems, around it. However, this may not last because of the heat of the pipe. In that case, you can force epoxy metal mender into the joint.

If the pipe sags, wrap a wire around it and tie it to a screw eye in the ceiling.

Holes in Stove Pipe

If there's one hole, there probably will soon be others; so good sense says to replace the pipe. However, you can plug holes temporarily by cleaning the metal and smearing on epoxy mender.

Cracks and Holes in a Stove

Don't use the stove till you have had a welder repair the damage.

11 Fuel for the Fire

If fireplaces ever again lose popularity in the United States, it will be because we've run out of firewood.

I agree that this sounds—and is—absurd. The United States may run out of other kinds of wood, but never firewood. No, what we shall run out of is the willingness to cut firewood.

We've become a nation of sluggards. If things don't come to us on a platter, to heck with them. When the fuel crisis hit us full force in 1974, and fireplaces suddenly took a big leap upward in popularity, the Connecticut government announced that anyone who wanted to go into the state forests and cut dead and fallen trees for firewood was welcome to do so.

I live on the edge of one of these forests and have yet to hear the sound of an ax or chain saw. This despite the fact that, with demand for wood soaring and the number of men cutting it falling, the price has gone through the roof. And the quality of the wood has dropped through the basement. Even in my area, where the forests are vast and thick, home owners have trouble buying really good firewood.

Choice of Woods

Thousands of learned words have been written about firewood—the good and the bad. But while the information they contain is of great value, much of it is rather academic.

The plain truth is that most people burn whatever wood is readily available at a reasonable price. If your property has more trees that you know what to do with, you probably cut them down and use them for firewood—even if it isn't very good firewood—in preference to spending money for neatly split oak. Similarly, if you live in an area that has little except pine, you're not too likely to pay for hickory imported from the other side of the state.

Another reason the technical facts about the BTU values of the different species of wood may be of minor importance to you is that you may not burn a fire so much for the heat as for the atmosphere it creates. A popping, crackling, spark-producing fire of pine may suit you a lot better than a quiet, hot fire of oak.

Be all this as it may, some knowledge of what constitutes good firewood is worth having, and here it is in a nutshell:

149

By and large, the heavier the wood, the more heat it produces and the longer it burns. The lighter the wood, the easier it is to ignite. The more resinous the wood, the better show it puts on—and the more likely it is to set your house on fire by shooting sparks onto the floor and rugs.

The characteristics of some of the most common wood species used for firewood are shown in the chart below:

FIREWOOD CHARACTERISTICS

Wood	Approx. Weight per Cu. Ft. of Seasoned Wood (Lbs.)	Available Heat per Cord (Millions of BTUs) Green	Dried	Starting Ease	Spark Output	Fragrance
Ash	40	16.5	20	Fair	Few	Slight
Beech	44	17.3	21.8	Poor	Few	Slight
Birch, white	38	17.3	21.3	Good	Moderate	Slight
Elm	35	14.3	17.2	Fair	Very few	Fair
Hickory	51	20.7	24.6	Fair	Moderate	Slight
Maple, sugar	44	18.4	21.3	Poor	Few	Good
Oak, red	44	17.9	21.3	Poor	Few	Fair
Pine, white	25	12.1	13.3	Excellent	Moderate	Good

To compare the heat output of these or any other species of wood with that of oil, divide the BTU value of a cord of wood by 140,000. This will tell you how many gallons of oil would be required to produce the same amount of heat. To make the same comparison with gas, divide the BTU value of wood by 100,000. This tells you how many therms of gas would be required.

Seasoning Wood You have undoubtedly heard it said that if you want a fire to burn longer you should mix some green wood with the seasoned wood. For fireplaces and simple stoves, this is good advice. But if you expect maximum heat from a fire, forget green wood. As the above chart indicates, seasoned wood, on average, produces 20 percent more heat than green wood. What's more, it isn't so hard to keep burning. Once ignited, it usually burns right down to ashes.

150

For wood to be adequately seasoned, it should be stacked and allowed to dry for six months. An extra six months produces even better firewood.

Wood will dry out and season if it is left out in the open. But the process is prolonged by rain and snow, and if you don't use up the wood within a year, it may start to rot. Punky and rotten wood makes rotten firewood. It follows that, if possible, the wood should be seasoned under some sort of shelter. If you can't do this, do at least stack the wood so the logs slant for water to run off rapidly.

Seasoning is also aided by stacking wood loosely so that air can circulate through it freely. Raise the stack off the ground several inches to let air pass underneath and to prevent the logs in the bottom layer from soaking up moisture from the ground and rotting out in short order.

The heating value of wood cut from dead trees as opposed to green wood that has been well seasoned is hard to determine. If the trees have been dead for only about a year, the wood is about the same as seasoned wood (assuming, of course, that it is not beginning to decay). But wood from trees that have been dead for several years is rarely the equal of six- to twelve-month-old seasoned wood, although it may give off considerable heat.

Bark on firewood gives off less heat than the wood and is consumed much more rapidly. But it is rarely practical to remove it; and since it does have some heating value, why should you?

Buying and Cutting Wood

Firewood is usually sold by the cord or fraction thereof. This is a stack of wood 8 feet long by 4 feet high by 4 feet wide. If well graded, it contains about 80 cubic feet of wood (and if you care to figure it out, about 58 cubic feet of air).

Sometimes, however, wood is sold by face cords measuring 8 feet long by 4 feet high by only 16 or 24 inches wide. You must be careful when buying a cord of wood that you don't actually receive a face cord, which contains only one-third or one-half of a cord, depending on the log length.

When people cut down trees and saw up their own firewood, the normal practice is to lop off the limbs immediately. This is all right to do in winter; but in summer, you will help to speed the seasoning process if you leave the limbs on the tree so the foliage can draw moisture from the wood. Then cut up the trees as soon as possible after the leaves wither. The reason for this haste is that

151

short lengths of wood dry faster than entire trunks. Split lengths dry even faster.

Every bit of wood is useful. The twigs can be used instead of newspaper to start fires. Small branches up to about one inch in diameter and chunks of loose bark make good kindling. And all the larger branches can be used either with the logs cut from the trunk or to feed fires that don't burn well.

Split logs catch fire more readily, burn more evenly and completely and are consumed faster by flames than unsplit logs. But there's a limit to how far you should go in splitting sections of trunk and heavy limbs. Generally, logs under four or five inches in diameter are left whole.

Splitting logs larger than this is a skill that can be acquired only by long practice. It isn't the safest of occupations. You need a long-handled ax, preferably weighing about five pounds, and it should be kept razor sharp. A dull ax is much more dangerous than a sharp one because it may bounce off a log and glance against your leg.

For very large or difficult logs, you need a steel wedge— preferably a pair of wedges—and a six-pound maul.

It's impossible to lay down any hard-and-fast rules about how you should strike a log with an ax, because that depends on the diameter of the log, the species of wood and whether the grain is straight or twisted. Small logs, however, are usually stood upright (make sure they stand firmly or are braced on two sides) and split from end to end. Larger logs, on the other hand, are usually laid flat or on a slight slant and struck on the side. In either case, if the wood is well seasoned and if you hit it in the right spot, it flies apart in two pieces. Elm logs are notable exceptions: they have such twisted fibers that you have to be a Lizzie Borden to split them.

Using a wedge is in some ways easier though the maul is more tiring to wield than an ax—and less fun. Lay the log flat; tap the wedge into the side, usually fairly close to the near end; and whale away. If it's a particularly ornery log, you will probably need to insert another wedge in the split started by the first.

I've never had any need for a log-splitter, but some people swear by them. They work in several ways; and there's no doubt that they take a big strain off the muscles, especially if you're splitting wood to heat the whole house. But they cost a hundred dollars up.

Ersatz Logs   Ersatz logs made of sawdust mixed with chemicals and pressed make beautiful firewood. They ignite immediately, without the aid of paper or kindling (partly because of the chemicals and partly because they come wrapped in paper); they give off plenty of heat (although how this compares with real wood, I don't know); and they burn a long time.

I make no claim to have timed how long compressed logs last, but when they first appeared on the market, it was my impression that they burned for three to four hours. The logs I've most recently used have a much shorter life. Check the labels to see if they indicate what the burning life of the logs is, and buy accordingly.

Because of the high cost of the logs, I wouldn't dream of relying on them exclusively. But if you can't lay hands on anything better, they're fine. They are also excellent for giving you a quick fire for about two or three hours.

There are three things about the logs you should watch out for, however: (1) if mixed with real wood, they'll produce a much bigger fire than is safe; (2) they should not be used in prefabricated built-in or free-standing fireplaces because their intense heat is likely to damage the metal; (3) you shouldn't roast marshmallows or cook over them because the chemicals imparted to the food are toxic.

Other Firewood Substitutes   The prettiest fires I've ever seen were made with driftwood, especially driftwood picked up along an ocean beach. After it has dried out, it burns with special vigor, putting out flames in every color. But it doesn't last long, so you are forever tossing more pieces into a fire to keep it going.

Tightly rolled newspapers have lately come into vogue as fire logs—largely, I suppose, because we have so many of them. But unless you have one of the gadgets designed to roll the papers, they are difficult to roll tightly enough to burn for any length of time. I don't know what their BTU value is. But I do know that, while they give off warmth, they don't make the same sort of soul-satisfying fire that real wood does. Even the *Wall Street Journal*, which several of my friends insist makes the best newspaper logs, is a pale imitation of a solid hickory log.

(Loose newspapers, scrap paper and cardboard should not be used to stoke a fire because they produce such flames that you're

153

in constant danger of starting a chimney fire. As for excelsior—never.)

Pine cones don't count as fuel because they're consumed too rapidly. But I know people who rely on them rather heavily—perhaps because they give a bright, often sparkling fire. They're best for kindling, however.

Storing Logs The best place to store logs is outdoors—either in the woodshed or in small piles on the porch where you can get at them easily. I'm not very happy about storing them indoors in a woodbox or the basement, because you can't be sure what sort of wood-eating insects—termites, carpenter ants, etc.—you may bring in with them.

Coal Two kinds of coal are used. Cannel coal goes into fireplaces; ordinary soft (bituminous) coal is used mainly in stoves, but to some extent in fireplaces.

Cannel coal is delightful. It comes in big but rather light-weight chunks that are relatively clean to handle. And it burns with tremendous vigor, giving off a lot of heat and flame at the same time. For years I used it in some fireplaces in preference to wood.

The trouble with the stuff is that it has become very expensive; and as it burns, it shatters into sheets with great popping noises and considerable flying debris. Actually, I don't recall that I ever saw a red-hot piece fly out onto the floor; but I give no guarantee that some of the pieces cannot start a fire. I can vouch for the fact that, after you've burned cannel coal throughout the evening, you'll find the floor strewn for yards around with black, unburned particles.

Soft coal is considerably dirtier to handle and gives off more soot. But it produces more heat—as well as more carbon monoxide. For the latter reason, when using it, you must provide an ample amount of air and must attend the fire constantly to assure that combustion is complete.

Storing Coal Since some coal may ignite spontaneously, it must be stored carefully.

It should be kept under cover so it doesn't get wet. The temperature of the storage area should be below 75 degrees. Avoid

154

storage close to heating pipes or ducts. And don't allow leaves, hay, grass clippings, bits of wood, cotton rags, papers and the like to accumulate in the coal pile.

Charcoal   I can't imagine anyone burning charcoal in a fireplace or stove for heat, because it's much too costly. But there are some who do so— at least occasionally.

There are also too many people who have burned charcoal— and died as a result. Despite its innocent appearance, it is a bountiful source of carbon monoxide. So if you ever do use it, give the fire plenty of air and make sure that the chimney flue is wide open.

12 Building and Tending Fires

Fire-building is not the exclusive province of the American male, but it comes close. And for many men there is a definite ritual to the operation. Which helps to explain why there is as much variation in fire-building "rules" as there is in martini-mixing "rules."

Whether you choose to develop and/or adopt some of these rules is entirely up to you. I confess I'm not much of a ritualist about fire-building or anything else. All I want to do is to get a fire laid so it will start off with a mild whoosh and keep on going. Much of my success—or lack of success—depends on how well seasoned the wood is to begin with.

Given good firewood, there isn't much of a problem about fire-building and tending. There are, however, several things that help.

1. It's generally best to use a pair of andirons spaced a foot to a foot and a half apart to raise the logs above the ashes so that air can flow freely under the fire. The andirons also keep round logs from rolling out onto the forehearth and beyond.

The alternative is to use a grate, or fire basket. In fact, for a coal fire you almost definitely require a grate.

(Incidentally, neither andirons nor grates are of much value if the legs break off. But there's no need to replace them when that happens. A local welding shop can repair the damage at relatively low cost.)

2. Keep a one- to two-inch bed of ashes on the hearth under the fire. It helps to insulate the cold hearth from the fire and make the fire easier to start.

3. You must make sure that the fire is getting enough air to maintain combustion. How to do this has been covered in other chapters.

The Starter Crumpled newspaper is the standard starter for ninety-nine out of one hundred fire-builders. But to get things off to a rousing start, the paper should be bone dry. If it sits around in a damp room for very long, it soaks up moisture and ignites reluctantly. Another trouble with newspaper is that it leaves a heavy, flaky ash which makes a messy-looking fireplace.

156

Building and tending fires

Use four or five sheets and crumple them pretty well so that they don't burn out before the kindling catches. You can also roll individual sheets diagonally from end to end and tie them into loose overhand knots.

If you prefer to recycle your newspapers and also to lay a prettier fire that produces less ash, you might follow the woodsman's practice of shaving down the corners of several sticks of pine or spruce kindling with a pocket knife. Make the shavings about $\frac{1}{16}$ to $\frac{1}{8}$ inch thick and 3 to 4 inches long, and don't break them off the stick. Just let them curl out to the sides in a fan.

A Cape Cod lighter is a nice touch, especially if you're an antiques enthusiast. This is a covered brass or iron container, filled with kerosene, that sits on the forehearth. Immersed in it is a more or less egg-shaped lump of soapstone or other porous material attached to a short handle. The lump soaks up the kerosene. To light the fire, touch a match to the lump and stick the lump under the kindling. Be sure it's cool before you put it back into the kerosene for a refill.

Less glamorous is an electric starter of the type used to start a charcoal fire for barbecuing. This must also be allowed to cool before you put it away after the fire is going.

Some people have a gas pipe built into the fireplace. They turn the valve, which is outside the fireplace, ignite the gas with a match and then let the gas burn till the fire is well started. It's easy and neat, but the pipe interferes to a certain extent with fire-building.

There are also chemical-saturated fiber pellets which you can buy for fire-starting. But they're no better than anything else and cost more.

Kindling Small branches that blow down out of trees in storms and that you collect from pruning solid-stemmed shrubs make as good kindling as anything and cost nothing. But they must, of course, be dry throughout. Not seasoned—just dry.

Old boards and timbers from whatever source are good, but only after you split them into sticks about $\frac{1}{4}$ to $\frac{3}{4}$ inch across.

The length of the branches and boards is not crucial. Twelve inches is a good average, however, since the sticks fit easily between andirons and can be arranged neatly in the fireplace.

Lay the sticks in criss-cross fashion on top of the newspapers. (If you use a grate, both sticks and newspapers can be in the grate or underneath.) Don't be reluctant to use plenty. On the other hand, there's no point in using too many. Eight or ten are usually enough to assure that the logs will be burning briskly by the time the kindling is consumed.

If you use pine cones as kindling—they're also good—just tumble them together in a loose pile.

Laying the Logs   Four or five logs are needed for a good fire. A lone log almost never gets started, and two aren't much better. Three usually work but the fire is likely to be sluggish.

The largest log should be placed near the back of the fireplace, but it must be spaced out from the wall at least half an inch. Some people prefer to place a very small log at the very back of the fireplace and put the big log in front of this. In either case, a smaller log is set in front of the big one. If both have straight sides, space them about an inch apart. Then lay the other logs in the chinks above. Now you're ready to light the fire.

Lighting the Fire   Open the damper before you do anything else. I recall the Sunday afternoon when I was confined to a chair with a broken ankle and my wife decided to warm up the living room for the benefit of several guests by starting the fire. It was the first fire we had ever had in the fireplace, because it was a brand-new house, and it got off to a wretched start. Within minutes the thick smoke that billowed out had everyone gasping. My wife and I looked at each other and almost in unison asked, "Do you think anything's wrong with the chimney?" And then immediately: "You (I) didn't open the damper!"

If the weather is cold, the chimney will be cold and cold air is likely to roll down into the fireplace when the damper is opened and fill the room with smoke when the fire is started. To prevent this, roll a sheet of newspaper into a loose roll, touch a match to one end and hold it up in the throat of the fireplace until the flames threaten to singe your hand. This will start the air flowing in the right direction.

Touch a match or the burning newspaper to the starter under the fire.

158

Tending the Fire

No one needs to be told how to tend a fire. That seems to come naturally to everyone. Most people, in fact, overtend a fire, but there is no great harm in that.

For a brisk fire, keep the logs pushed together fairly close. (This is called "kissing" by Down East old-timers.) If a new log is called for, put it on before the others burn away so much that they don't produce enough flame to get it started. As the evening wears on, if you want to get most of the wood on the fire burned up, keep piling the pieces on top of one another.

If the fire threatens to die down before the fuel is consumed, pull away the firescreen so it gets more air. If this doesn't work, open a window a crack.

The poker may be the tool you use most to push and pull logs around, but tongs are needed frequently, too. Most tongs aren't worth the price you pay for them. They may be flimsy. And the standard tongs with only two straight legs are hard to use for lifting logs. A more efficient design has rounded claws that fit around a log. One is a single claw; the other is split into a wide V. If you use the tongs with the V claw on the underside, you can lift logs without having to balance them nicely in the tongs.

Putting Out Fires

If you go to bed or leave home before the fire is out, it's unwise to let it burn away merrily because you can't be certain that a spark won't fly out or a log roll forward into the room, whether you have a screen or not. There's no need, however, to wet the fire down. Just pick the logs up with your tongs and stand them in the back corners of the firebox. They should be set at a safe angle so they can't fall and roll out into the room. The flames will soon die out. Be sure to put the firescreen in place before leaving the room; and don't close the damper until the fire is dead. (Incidentally, you should also make sure a fire is dead before laying a new one; otherwise, the new one may go up in smoke before you want it to.)

One of my thrifty friends goes one step further in extinguishing fires. After stacking the logs in the corners of the firebox, he closes off the opening with a sheet of asbestos-cement board. Thus the house heat is not sucked up the chimney during the night.

Banking Fires   If you burn a fire continuously, the only way to carry it through the night so it will burst almost immediately into flame the next morning is to cover the burning logs with ashes just before you retire. Keep the damper open and don't cover the fireplace opening as suggested above. The logs will continue to give off some heat to the room; and when you pull away the ashes in the morning, there will be glowing coals.

Managing Coal Fires   Coal gives off killing amounts of carbon monoxide if the fire is not attended faithfully.

You can start a coal fire with paper alone, but paper and a few sticks of kindling give faster results. As the fire burns along, a thick bed of glowing coals is produced. New lumps of coal should be added while the old coals are still very active. If they cool and become covered with ash, they will increase production of gases and new coals will not be ignited so rapidly. They may, in fact, explode (although there is rarely any great danger when this happens).

If you do let coals burn down before adding fresh fuel, you should first toss in some paper and kindling to get the new lumps going quickly.

The air supply must be maintained at all times. *Never, never, never* close the damper until a coal fire is completely extinguished.

Overfiring and Underfiring   Whatever fuel you burn, it is important to maintain a moderately vigorous fire. If the fire is underfired—too cool—the volatile substances given off will probably condense in the cool flue and build up on the flue walls. This build-up not only can affect combustion in the firebox but may also ignite when you build up a fire too high.

Overfiring causes ignition of the soot in the flue and sometimes cracks the flue and chimney or gets it so hot that the surrounding wood-framing members burst into flame.

Chimney Fires   If you ever do have a chimney fire, call the fire department at once. While you're waiting for the trucks to appear, you should try to extinguish the fire in the fireplace with water (but take care, if using a hose, not to squirt water up the chimney, because this could crack the lining). Then cover the fireplace opening with a damp blanket or rug to keep out air.

160

In a stove, a fire can be extinguished or at least controlled by sprinkling it with a large quantity of salt—preferably rock salt.

Final Word of Warning Never under any circumstances try to start a fire or feed a sluggish fire with kerosene, gasoline or other inflammable liquid!

13 This, That and the Other Thing

Buying a House with a Fireplace

When you buy an old house, you're never quite sure about its condition; and being something of a connoisseur of old houses, I am even more uncertain about the condition of the fireplaces.

You ask the previous owner: "Is it a good fireplace?"

"Oh, yes, it's a fine fireplace."

But is it or isn't it? Unless you press on with your questioning —and most home buyers don't—you don't know when the previous owner last used the fireplace, how often he used it, whether the chimney has ever been cleaned—all sorts of things that would give you a better idea of what "a fine fireplace" really means.

I'm the trusting type about most things, but not fireplaces. Fireplaces are a potential hazard. So whatever you're told about the fireplace in a house you buy, check it out a little before you start using it.

Rattle the damper open and shut a few times to see how much soot is dislodged. Get down into the fireplace for a look up the chimney. If it's angled, you'll need a flashlight and you'll also have to get up on the roof and look down. Are the walls of the flue encrusted with carbon? Do you see any bulging flue tiles? Any loose bricks?

Examine the fireplace, too, though unless it's filled with ashes, a quick glance pretty well tells the story.

If you don't like the looks of anything, get a chimney cleaner to clean the chimney and tell you what, if anything, he finds wrong with it. You may then need to call in a mason to double-check and make repairs. In the meantime, try to avoid using the fireplace; and if you use it at all, use it cautiously. Keep your fires small. Above all, don't use the fireplace as an incinerator for all the packing materials that move in with you.

Opening a Boarded-up Fireplace

When fireplaces went out of style years ago, many of them were boarded up, bricked in or plastered over to keep from wasting heat. Now, of course, most home owners want them; yet they are slightly hesitant about reopening them.

Remember this: Just because a fireplace was closed up in, say,

1909 doesn't mean there was anything wrong with it then or that there's anything wrong with it now. Nevertheless, since you don't know exactly why it was closed up or what toll time has taken, it's wise to assume the worst and hire a fireplace expert to give the whole thing a good going-over before you burn your first fire in it.

Heat Boosters Ever since the energy crisis started, would-be inventors have had a field day trying to develop something that would extract more heat from fireplaces. To date, none of them has been overwhelmingly successful—probably because all of them are thinking along the same line. But at least they have made some progress.

Whatever the fancy names given to them, heat boosters are, with two exceptions, glorified fireplace grates that take in cold air from the room, circulate it around the fire and return heated air to the room. Thus they work like circulating fireplaces.

In the simplest boosters, the grates are made of steel tubes that form a large U around the fire. These depend entirely on natural air circulation. In more elaborate boosters, the cold air is pulled into the grate by a small electric fan placed to one side of the fireplace; thus air movement and the amount of extra heat given off by the booster are increased slightly.

To my knowledge, no objective scientific test has been made to evaluate the effectiveness of heat boosters. The only thing you have to go on are the manufacturer's own studies, which are hardly unbiased and are probably not very thorough or scientific. For whatever it's worth, one of these studies shows that without a heat booster, a fireplace alone raised the temperature in a 15 x 26-foot room from a starting point of 52 degrees to 67 and 56 degrees after two hours. The higher temperature was recorded at a point 6 feet from the fireplace; the lower, at a point 26 feet from the fireplace. By comparison, the same fireplace with a fan-equipped booster raised the temperature from 52 to 75 degrees at 6 feet and 73 degrees at 26 feet.

Even if you cut these heat-gains in half, it's apparent that this particular booster at least does a pretty good job.

The two heat boosters that operate in a different manner are a chimney-heat reclaimer and a water-circulating booster.

The heat reclaimer is similar to those used on central heating systems. It's a fairly small device which is built into the flue pipe

Most heat boosters are constructed more or less like this. Cool air flows in through the tubes at the bottom, and as it circulates through them, it is heated and flows out at the top. Such units can usually be equipped with a fan to speed air circulation.
(Thermograte Enterprises)

In this fan-forced heat booster, air enters the long box at the near end and flows back through the right tube (partially hidden by screen) into a metal box under the grate, where it is heated. It then flows back into the room through the left tube and slots in front of the long box. (Metal Concepts)

just above free-standing fireplaces and stoves, and it's designed to capture and circulate into the room some of the heat that is normally wasted up the flue. A built-in circulating fan spreads the captured heat across the room. There's also a thermostat that turns the booster on and off.

The water-circulating booster is a grate connected to a central hot-water heating plant. When the fireplace is in use, water flowing through the grate is heated and returned to the boiler, from which it is then circulated to the radiators throughout the house. The manufacturer also produces a complete water-circulating fireplace designed for installation in a masonry fireplace.

165

Designed for stoves and fireplaces with metal flues, this heat reclaimer uses the flue gases to heat fresh air which is blown through heat-exchanger tubes into the room. (Calcinator)

Firebacks   In days gone by, many fireplaces had a cast-iron slab that was set into the back of the firebox to radiate extra heat into the room and at the same time protect the masonry. Many of these firebacks, as they were called, were embossed with ornamental designs.

I don't know of any firms that produce firebacks today; but if you want one, you can have it made to order of cast iron or steel by a metal-working shop. For maximum effectiveness, it should be bent or curved to conform to the existing masonry back.

Firescreens   For safety, every fireplace should have a firescreen. Not that a screen is a 100 percent guarantee against the escape of sparks; but it does reduce the chances of sparks setting fire to the floor beyond the forehearth.

The least effective firescreen is the folding type which is placed on the forehearth several inches out from the fireplace opening. It will contain sparks that fly straight out from the fire but does nothing about those that vault up and out like a high-jumper.

To stop all kinds of sparks, a firescreen should completely cover the fireplace opening and fit tight against the four sides of the opening. Two kinds of free-standing screens meet these requirements. One is flat—either a rigid screen or a drawn screen hung within a four-sided frame. The other is shaped like an old-fashioned coal shovel or sometimes like a wedge. This stands out from the fireplace about eight inches but has a hood at the top and wings at the sides that press against the surround. The two types of screen are equally effective in stopping sparks; but the flat type is more easily knocked over by rolling logs unless the uprights of the andirons are placed in front of the screen (as they sometimes are in draw-type flat screens).

Built-in firescreens are a bit more attractive than free-standing screens because they don't conceal the edges of the opening; and you don't have to move them out of the way when you build or tend the fire or want to enjoy the fire without a screen. But the popular draw-screen type of built-in is a little less safe than a flat or hooded free-standing screen because there's an open crack at the bottom and, unless you take pains to spread the flexible screens, there may be cracks at the sides and in the middle. Furthermore, rolling logs can roll right under the screen.

Draw screens work like draw draperies. Depending on the de-

167

Identical fireplaces—one in the dining-kitchen area, the other in the living room. The screens are of the hooded type but are triangular in cross-section. This not only gives them a more modern appearance but also makes them harder to tip over.

Glass firescreens are safer than mesh and help to prevent heat loss when the fireplace is not in use.

sign, you can push the screens apart by hand or pull them open and closed with pull chains. One type—the better looking, in my opinion—is recessed just inside the fireplace opening, with the track in which the screens slide anchored to the lintel. The other type—a little safer—overlaps the top and sides of the fireplace opening an inch or two.

Another kind of built-in screen is a roll-down unit that is hidden behind the lintel when not in use and pulls down—like a window shade—when the fire is burning. It is little known, but should be more widely used because it doesn't mar the appearance of the fireplace.

Glass built-in screens are the safest of all because sparks cannot possibly get through them. They also help to reduce the loss of heat up the chimney when the fireplace is not in use. But while they allow you to watch the fire, they deprive you of its aroma and sound. And they cut down the amount of heat you receive from the fire to some extent.

A glass screen consists of a four-sided frame overlapping the fireplace opening, and a pair of tempered-glass doors. Air is introduced from the room to the fire through an ornamental adjustable grille in the base of the frame. A flexible draw screen can be added inside the doors so you can open the doors without fear of escaping sparks.

14 Who Makes It?

Masonry Fireplace Parts (Dampers, Ash Dumps, Spark Arresters, etc.)

Heatilator Div.
Vega Industries, Inc.
Mt. Pleasant, Iowa 52641

Majestic Co.
Huntington, Ind. 46750

Superior Fireplace Co.
4325 Artesia Ave.
Fullerton, Calif. 92633

Vestal Manufacturing Co.
Box 420
Sweetwater, Tenn. 37874

Mantels and Mantel Shelves

Barclay Industries, Inc.
65 Industrial Rd.
Lodi, N.J. 07644
(Shelves)

Fair-Fold, Inc.
East Farmingdale, N.Y. 11735
(Shelves)

Focal Point, Inc.
3760 Lower Roswell Rd.
Marietta, Ga. 30060

Edwin Jackson, Inc.
306 E. 61st St.
New York, N.Y. 10021

Morgan Co.
Oshkosh, Wis. 54901

Francis J. Purcell II
Box 7, RD 2
New Hope, Pa. 18938

Sears Roebuck (Shelves)

Hoods

Goodwin of California, Inc.
1075 Second St.
Berkeley, Calif. 94710
(Hoods for Island Fireplaces)

A.C. Hathorne Co.
55 San Remo Dr.
South Burlington, Vt. 05401

Fireplace Facings

Acorn Building Components, Inc.
12620 Westwood
Detroit, Mich. 48223

Buckingham-Virginia Slate Corp.
4110 Fitzhugh Ave.
Richmond, Va. 23230

Vermont Marble Co.
Proctor, Vt. 05765

Circulating Fireplaces

General Products Co.
Box 887
Fredericksburg, Va. 22401

Heatilator Div.
Vega Industries, Inc.
Mt. Pleasant, Iowa 52641

Majestic Co.
Huntington, Ind. 46750

Superior Fireplace Co.
4325 Artesia Ave.
Fullerton, Calif. 92633

Vestal Manufacturing Co.
Box 420
Sweetwater, Tenn. 37874

Prefabricated Built-in Fireplaces

Heatilator Div.
Vega Industries, Inc.
Mt. Pleasant, Iowa 52641

Majestic Co.
Huntington, Ind. 46750

Martin Industries, Inc.
Box 1527
Huntsville, Ala. 35807

Montgomery Ward

Preway, Inc.
Wisconsin Rapids, Wis. 54494

Temco, Inc.
4104 Charlotte Ave.
Nashville, Tenn. 37202

A.R. Wood Manufacturing Co.
Box 218
Luverne, Minn. 56156

Free-standing Fireplaces

Atlanta Stove Works
Box 5254
Atlanta, Ga. 30307

Goodwin of California, Inc.
1075 Second St.
Berkeley, Calif. 94710

Gordon Corp.
504 Main St.
Farmington, Conn. 06032

Kristia Associates
449 Forest Ave.
Portland, Me. 04104

Lau Industries Div.
Philips Industries, Inc.
2027 Home Ave.
Dayton, Ohio 45407

Majestic Co.
Huntington, Ind. 46750

Malm Fireplaces, Inc.
368 Yolanda Ave.
Santa Rosa, Calif. 95404

Martin Industries, Inc.
Box 1527
Huntsville, Ala. 35807

Montgomery Ward

Preway, Inc.
Wisconsin Rapids, Wis. 54494

Southport Stoves
248 Tolland St.
East Hartford, Conn. 06108

Superior Fireplace Co.
4325 Artesia Ave.
Fullerton, Calif. 92633

Temco, Inc.
4104 Charlotte Ave.
Nashville, Tenn. 37202

A.R. Wood Manufacturing Co.
Box 218
Luverne, Minn. 56156

Electric Fireplaces

Cavrok Corp.
Industrial Park Ave.
Vernon, Conn. 06066

Fasco Industries, Inc.
Fayetteville, N.C. 28302

Leigh Products, Inc.
Coopersville, Mich. 49404

Majestic Co.
Huntington, Ind. 46750

Martin Industries, Inc.
Box 1527
Huntsville, Ala. 35807

Miami-Carey Co.
203 Garver Rd.
Monroe, Ohio 45050

Montgomery Ward

Gas-burning Fireplaces

Majestic Co.
Huntington, Ind. 46750

Martin Industries, Inc.
Box 1527
Huntsville, Ala. 35807

Preway, Inc.
Wisconsin Rapids, Wis. 54494

Temco, Inc.
4101 Charlotte Ave.
Nashville, Tenn. 37202

Stoves

Autocrat Corp.
New Athens, Ill. 62264

C & D Distributors, Inc.
Box 766
Old Saybrook, Conn. 06475

Empire Stove Co.
Belleville, Ill. 62222

Fire-View Distributors
Box 370
Rogue River, Ore. 97537

Kickapoo Stove Works
Main St.
LaFarge, Wis. 54639

King Products Div.
Martin Industries, Inc.
Box 730
Sheffield, Ala. 35660

Kristia Associates
449 Forest Ave.
Portland, Me. 04103

Mohawk Industries, Inc.
173 Howland Ave.
Adams, Mass. 01220

Monarch Kitchen Appliances
Beaver Dam, Wis. 53916

Montgomery Ward

Portland Stove Foundry
Box 1156
Portland, Me. 04104

Scandinavian Stoves, Inc.
Box 72, Rte. 12A
Alstead, N.H. 03602

Self-Sufficiency Products
1 Appletree Square
Minneapolis, Minn. 55420

Southport Stoves
248 Tolland St.
East Hartford, Conn. 06108

Vermont Castings, Inc.
Randolph, Vt. 05060

Prefabricated Chimneys

General Products Co.
Box 887
Fredericksburg, Va. 22401

Hart & Cooley Manufacturing Co.
Box 903A
Holland, Mich. 49423

Wallace-Murray Corp.
3 Gateway Center
Pittsburgh, Pa. 15222

Heat Boosters

Aquappliances, Inc.
135 Sunshine Lane
San Marcos, Calif. 92069

Calcinator Corp.
28th and Water Sts.
Bay City, Mich. 48706

General Products Corp.
150 Ardale St.
West Haven, Conn. 06516

Metal Concepts, Inc.
Box 25596
Seattle, Wash. 98125

Ridgway Steel Fabricators, Inc.
Box 382
Ridgway, Pa. 15853

Stites Manufacturing Co.
615 Hunter Lane
Santa Rosa, Calif. 95404

Tel-O-Post Co.
Box 217
Linesville, Pa. 16424

Thermalite Corp.
Box 69
Hanover, Mass. 02339

Thermograte Enterprises, Inc.
51 Iona Lane
St. Paul, Minn. 55117

Draft Inducers

Field Control Div.
Conco
Mendota, Ill. 61342

Tjernlund Products, Inc.
1620 Terrace Dr.
St. Paul, Minn. 55113

Log-splitters

C & D Distributors, Inc.
Box 766
Old Saybrook, Conn. 06475

Conway Tractor & Equipment
Box 371
North Conway, N.H. 03860

Futura Master Corp.
5069 Highway 45 S
West Bend, Wis. 53095

Index